Ladies' Home Journal
Easy as 1-2-3
COOKBOOK LIBRARY

Ladies' Home Journal

Easy as 1-2-3

ENTERTAINING COOKBOOK

by the Editors of Ladies' Home Journal

PUBLISHED BY LADIES' HOME JOURNAL BOOKS

Ladies' Home Journal

Myrna Blyth, Editor-in-Chief
Sue B. Huffman, Food Editor
Jan T. Hazard, Associate Food Editor
Tamara Schneider, Art Director

Produced in association with Media Projects Incorporated

Carter Smith, Executive Editor
Ellen Coffey, Senior Project Editor
Donna Ryan, Project Editor
Bernard Schleifer, Design Consultant
Design by Bruce Glassman

Manufactured in the United States of America
Library of Congress Cataloging-in-Publication Data
Main entry under title:
Ladies' home journal easy as 1-2-3 entertaining cookbook.
Includes index.
1. Cookery. 2. Entertaining. I. Ladies' home journal.
TX652.L2253 1985   641.5   85-25229
ISBN 0-935639-03-9

Preface

I think most of us wish we had more time to entertain, to have friends and family for dinner more often, but we don't have the time for the elaborate preparations for guests. And so another month or season or even year goes by. Yet we could entertain a lot more if we realized that there are many delicious meals that take a minimum of time and preparation.

What's the key to company-perfect meals anyone can make? Choosing the right menu—appropriate for guests yet at the same time quick and easy.

Ease of preparation is indeed the basis of this Easy as 1-2-3 Entertaining Cookbook. *You'll notice that each menu gives you a shopping list so that you know exactly what to buy as well as a list of staples to have on hand. Our staff has worked out a schedule, too, so that you know exactly what you need to do step by step as you prepare a meal you can serve to your guests with pride. We've also included countless tips throughout the book, to help give the appropriately festive finishing touches that dress up countless dishes.*

What's the real *aim of this book? To turn entertaining from a worrisome chore to a simple pleasure, and to enable you to see the people you want to see a lot more often. Our* Ladies' Home Journal *guarantee is that with the* Easy as 1-2-3 Entertaining Cookbook *in your kitchen, from now on you'll be greeting your guests at the door with a relaxed smile on your face.*

Myrna Blyth
Editor-in-Chief
Ladies' Home Journal

Contents

Fresh Fillets Sauteed with Almonds 30
Trout Amandine, Creamed New Potatoes with Peas, Broiled Tomato Halves with Parsley, Ambrosia

A Flavorful Main Dish 36
Turkey with Cumin Sauce, Herbed Zucchini, Sesame Seed Bread, Mint Dreams

Easy Elegance for Enjoyable Entertaining 38
Asparagus Vinaigrette, Veal Cutlets with Mushroom Sauce, Rice with Parsley, Dilled Carrots, Coffee Ice Cream with Coffee Liqueur and Walnuts

Saucy French Chicken with Grapes 42
Chicken Veronique, Clove-Seasoned Rice, Spinach and Bean Sprout Salad, Butterscotch Parfaits

Italian Menu on the Light Side 44
Antipasto, Linguine with Spinach-Walnut Sauce, Italian Bread, Chicory and Tomato Salad, Chocolate Love

Fuss-Free Summer or Winter Dinner 46
Guacamole with Tortilla Chips, Barbecued Steak, Parsley Potatoes, Tossed Salad with Classic Dressing, Fruit-Topped Cheesecake

Dinner for a Festive Evening 48
Caviar-Topped New Potatoes, Chicken with Sherry, Rice, Fresh Zucchini Medley, Pecan Pie with Whipped Cream

An Elegant Company Dinner 50
Prosciutto-Wrapped Breadsticks, Veal Piccata, Fresh Asparagus Tips, Hard Rolls, Tomato Wedges and Marinated Artichoke Hearts on Red Lettuce, Quick Cherries Jubilee

Tender Cube Steak in Sour Cream Sauce 54
Beef Stroganoff, Egg Noodles, Cucumber-Onion-Tomato Salad, French Bread with Butter, Black Forest Sundaes

Celebrate with a Chanukah Dinner 56
Sweet and Sour Beef, Potato Latkes, Carrots, Holiday Red Cabbage, Honey Cake

Dinner with a Sweetheart Dessert 58
Chicken Breasts Amandine, Fuss-Free Risotto, Buttered Green Beans, Quick Cherry Crisp

Light, Just Right Company Dinner 62
Skewered Shrimp, Piquant Rice, Stir-Fried Snow Peas, Lemon Sherbet with Kiwi Slices

Perennial Favorites at Their Best 66
Pork Chops with Lime Sauce, Cranberry Fruit Relish, Fine Egg Noodles, Peppery Brussels Sprouts, Walnut Cake

Introduction

To set the scene: The table is laid with your best china and crystal. White wine is chilling in the fridge. Your first guests arrive with flowers, which are plunked (artfully) into a vase. With cocktails you bring out breadsticks, cleverly wrapped in prosciutto. Dinner is served: Veal Piccata, Fresh Asparagus, Tomatoes and Marinated Artichoke Hearts on Leaf Lettuce, Hot Rolls. At dessert time you bring the chafing dish to the table and prepare Cherries Jubilee with a flourish—in mere minutes. Brava for the hostess!

Scene two: A more informal setting. Pottery and country placemats. Start with Guacamole and Tortilla Chips, served perhaps with margaritas or mugs of beer. Then Barbecued Steak, Parsley Potatoes, Tossed Salad with Classic Dressing. The irresistible finale: Fruit-Topped Cheesecake. Olé for the hostess!

Entertaining takes hours, right? Wrong! Not with the Easy as 1-2-3 Entertaining Cookbook. *These menus and thirty-four others can be pulled off in half an hour. Now there's time to have a quick, relaxing soak and to redo your face from scratch before guests (long-invited or last-minute) knock at your door.*

What else can you serve? How about Skewered Shrimp, Piquant Rice, Stir-Fried Snow Peas, Lemon Sherbet with Kiwi Fruit? Or Zucchini Pizzas, Spaghetti Carbonara, Breadsticks, Arugula and Romaine Salad, and Fresh Fruit with Marsala? Smashing!

And as your guests rave and declare, "You must have spent hours on dinner," you can smile demurely and protest, "It was nothing!"

Sue B. Huffman
Food Editor
Ladies' Home Journal

Rosemary Pork Chops

HEARTY DINNER WITH A SPECIAL DESSERT

Here is a dinner which features a rich torte of pound cake layered with a creamy ricotta-chocolate filling—the ideal way to end this deliciously seasoned pork meal. Thinly sliced chops cut down on cooking time and when you're in a rush, that pound cake tucked in the freezer always comes in handy.

Menu for 6

- **Rosemary Pork Chops**
- **Potatoes l'Anglaise**
- **Green Beans with Pimiento Strips**
- **Cassata Torte**

SHOPPING LIST

- 6 loin pork chops
- 1 bunch fresh parsley
- 6 baking potatoes
- 1½ pounds fresh green beans
- 1 4-ounce jar pimientos
- 1 6-ounce package chocolate chips
- 1 pound cake
- 1 8-ounce container ricotta cheese

Have on Hand
- Sugar
- Salt
- Pepper
- Rosemary
- Garlic
- Olive oil

SCHEDULE

1. Prepare Rosemary Pork Chops.
2. Cook Potatoes l'Anglaise.
3. Prepare green beans.
4. Assemble Cassata Torte.

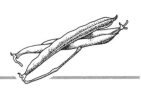

Rosemary Pork Chops

3   tablespoons olive oil
1½   teaspoons rosemary, crushed
1   garlic clove, minced
1   teaspoon salt
¼   teaspoon pepper
6   loin pork chops

In small bowl mix oil, rosemary, garlic, salt and pepper. Brush mixture on both sides of pork chops and broil about 6 inches from heat for 5 to 7 minutes on each side, or until cooked through.

Potatoes l'Anglaise

6   baking potatoes, peeled
     Water
     Salt
1   tablespoon butter or margarine
2   tablespoons chopped parsley

Quarter potatoes lengthwise, then cut in half crosswise. Trim edges to form football-shaped chunks. Heat 1 inch salted water to boiling; add potatoes and cook 10 to 12 minutes or until fork tender. Drain, toss with butter or margarine, place in serving dish; sprinkle with parsley.

Cassata Torte

1   cup ricotta cheese
¼   cup chocolate chips
3   tablespoons sugar
1   pound cake

In small bowl combine ricotta cheese with chocolate chips and sugar. Slice pound cake into 3 horizontal layers. Spread one third of filling on each layer. Stack layers and cut into slices.

EASY WAY TO SPLIT A POUND CAKE

Turn an everyday pound cake into a company-special treat any day by splitting it into layers and filling with custard, berries, sliced peaches, whipped cream or liqueur-spiked preserves. To split evenly, insert toothpicks in straight horizontal lines around sides of cake. Using the toothpicks as a guide, cut cake into layers with a long, serrated knife.

Sirloin with Bearnaise Sauce

A GALA MEAL ANY TIME OF YEAR

Please your guests with tender pan-broiled steak served with a tarragon-and-shallot-flavored sauce.

Menu for 6

Nut-Coated
Cheese Ball
Wheat Crackers
• Sirloin with
Bearnaise
Sauce

• Roasted
Potatoes
Sliced Tomatoes
and Onions
with Oil and
Vinegar

• Fresh Strawberry Sundaes

SHOPPING LIST

- [ ] 4   to 5 pounds sirloin steak, 1 inch thick
- [ ] 1   large shallot
- [ ] 4   tomatoes
- [ ] 1   bunch green onions
- [ ] 24 small new potatoes (about 3 pounds)
- [ ] 2   pints strawberries
- [ ] 1   package wheat crackers
- [ ] 1   nut-coated cheese ball

Have on Hand

- [ ]   Sugar
- [ ]   Salt ·
- [ ]   Pepper
- [ ]   Garlic
- [ ]   Dried tarragon
- [ ]   Dried rosemary
- [ ] 1 lemon or lemon juice
- [ ]   Salad oil
- [ ]   Wine vinegar
- [ ]   Eggs
- [ ]   Butter or margarine
- [ ]   Almond extract

SCHEDULE

1. Prepare Roasted Potatoes.
2. Make sauce for Fresh Strawberry Sundaes; refrigerate.
3. Prepare salad.
4. Prepare Sirloin with Bearnaise Sauce.

Sirloin with Bearnaise Sauce

4   to 5 pounds sirloin, about 1 inch thick
1   teaspoon salt
⅛   teaspoon pepper
½   cup wine vinegar
2   tablespoons chopped shallots
½   teaspoon dried tarragon
4   egg yolks
1   cup hot melted butter

Score fat on steak to prevent curling. Heat heavy skillet and brown steak quickly on both sides. Lower heat and add salt and pepper. Cook uncovered, pouring off fat that accumulates, about 3 minutes on each side for rare, 6 minutes for well done.

To make the Bearnaise Sauce, in small saucepan combine vinegar, shallots and tarragon. Cook over high heat until mixture is reduced to about 2 tablespoons. Place egg yolks in blender container. Pour in about ¼ cup melted butter and blend on high about 30 seconds. Continue adding butter slowly until all is incorporated. Add reduced vinegar and blend just until mixed. Pour a small amount of sauce over steak; serve remainder on the side.

Roasted Potatoes

3   tablespoons salad oil
1½   tablespoons butter or margarine
24   small new potatoes (about 3 lbs.)
1   clove garlic, pressed
2½   teaspoons rosemary, dried or fresh
½   teaspoon salt
¼   teaspoon pepper

Preheat oven to 400° F. In a square roasting pan combine oil and butter or margarine. Heat in oven 3 minutes to melt butter. Add potatoes and garlic. Sprinkle rosemary, salt and pepper over potatoes. Shake pan to coat potatoes evenly. Bake 25 to 30 minutes, shaking pan occasionally so potatoes will brown on all sides.

Fresh Strawberry Sundaes

2   pints strawberries, hulled and sliced
½   cup sugar
1½   tablespoons lemon juice
¼   teaspoon almond extract
1   quart vanilla ice cream

In saucepan combine strawberries, sugar, lemon juice and almond extract. Bring to a boil, reduce heat and simmer 10 minutes. Remove from heat; stir in almond extract. Refrigerate until serving time. Spoon over dishes of vanilla ice cream.

THE VARIETIES OF VINEGAR

For salads choose from the wine vinegars, which include pungent red wine vinegar and light, clear white wine vinegar as well as rice wine vinegars.

Turkey Cutlets à l'Orange

FAST AND FRUITY — DELICIOUS, TOO

An orange-flavored sauce adds interest to this turkey entree, served with a raisin-studded rice pilaf and fresh green beans. If you're planning this meal for a cold winter evening, serve the Cherry Cobbler piping hot from the oven—a sure way to warm your guests.

Menu for 6

- **Turkey Cutlets à l'Orange**
- **Rice Pilaf**

Green Beans
- **Quick Cherry Cobbler**

SHOPPING LIST

- ☐ 1½ pounds turkey cutlets
- ☐ 1½ pounds green beans
- ☐ 2 13¾- or 14½-ounce cans chicken broth
- ☐ 2 21-ounce cans cherry pie filling
- ☐ 1 8-ounce package refrigerated biscuits
- ☐ ½ pint heavy or whipping cream

Have on Hand
- ☐ Long-grain rice
- ☐ Brown sugar or cinnamon sugar

- ☐ Salt
- ☐ Pepper
- ☐ Ground cardamom or allspice
- ☐ Ground ginger
- ☐ Butter or margarine
- ☐ Dark seedless raisins
- ☐ Orange juice

SCHEDULE

1. Prepare Quick Cherry Cobbler.
2. Prepare Rice Pilaf.
3. Prepare green beans.
4. Prepare Turkey Cutlets à l'Orange.

Turkey Cutlets à l'Orange

3   tablespoons butter or
        margarine
1½   pounds turkey cutlets
½   teaspoon salt
        Dash pepper
¾   cup orange juice
¾   cup heavy or whipping
        cream
⅛   teaspoon ground carda-
        mom or allspice
⅛   teaspoon ginger

In large skillet melt butter or margarine over low heat. Sprinkle cutlets with salt and pepper. Increase heat to medium-high and quickly brown cutlets about 2 minutes on each side. Transfer to heated platter; keep warm. Combine orange juice, cream and spices; pour into skillet and cook just until sauce thickens slightly, 3 to 5 minutes. Add cutlets to sauce; heat through.

Rice Pilaf

3   cups chicken broth
1⅓   cups water
½   teaspoon salt
2   tablespoons butter or
        margarine
1½   cups long-grain rice
¼   cup dark seedless
        raisins

In heavy saucepan combine broth, water, salt and butter or margarine; bring to a boil. Stir in rice and raisins. Reduce heat to very low; cover and let cook until liquid is absorbed, 20 to 25 minutes.

Quick Cherry Cobbler

2   cans (21-oz. each) cherry
        pie filling
1   package (8 oz.) refriger-
        ated biscuits
¼   cup butter or margarine,
        melted
½   cup light brown sugar or
        cinnamon sugar

Preheat oven to 400° F. In medium sauce-pan heat cherry pie filling; transfer to ovenproof casserole.
   Roll refrigerated biscuits in melted butter, then in brown sugar or cinnamon sugar. Place on cherry pie filling. Bake 20 to 25 minutes.

QUICK SURPRISES WITH RAISINS

- *Combine dark seedless raisins with cream cheese as a spread.*
- *Mix with chopped ham and sauteed chopped onion; add to baked beans.*
- *Add to bread stuffing for poultry along with equal amounts chopped apple and pine nuts.*

Sesame Chicken

AN EASY AND APPEALING COMPANY MEAL

Whip up a batch of our quick Strawberry Mousse and pop it into the freezer. Then put together a crunchy chicken entree and its garlicky tomato-escarole accompaniment—a meal you will enjoy as much as your guests.

Menu for 6

- **Sesame Chicken**
- **Rice**

- **Sauteed Escarole and Cherry Tomatoes**

- **Strawberry Mousse**

SHOPPING LIST

- ☐ 6 chicken cutlets
- ☐ 2 heads (about 2 pounds) escarole
- ☐ 1 pint cherry tomatoes
- ☐ 1 jar sesame seed
- ☐ 1 pint heavy or whipping cream
- ☐ 2 10-ounce packages quick-thaw frozen strawberries

- ☐ Salad oil
- ☐ Olive oil
- ☐ Garlic
- ☐ Eggs
- ☐ Milk
- ☐ Butter or margarine

Have on Hand
- ☐ All-purpose flour
- ☐ Long-grain rice
- ☐ Salt ·
- ☐ Pepper
- ☐ Dried bread crumbs
- ☐ 1 lemon or Lemon juice

SCHEDULE

1. Prepare Strawberry Mousse; place in freezer.
2. Cook orzo.
3. Blanch escarole; drain.
4. Prepare Sesame Chicken.
5. Prepare Sauteed Escarole and Cherry Tomatoes.

Sesame Chicken

6   *chicken cutlets*
½   *cup all-purpose flour*
2   *eggs*
½   *cup milk*
¾   *cup dried bread crumbs*
½   *cup sesame seed*
1   *teaspoon salt*
¼   *teaspoon pepper*
2   *tablespoons salad oil*

Sprinkle chicken lightly with flour; set aside. In shallow bowl beat eggs and milk; set aside. In another shallow bowl combine bread crumbs, sesame seed, salt and pepper. Dip chicken into egg mixture and then into bread crumbs, coating both sides.

In large skillet heat oil over medium-high heat. Add chicken cutlets and cook 5 minutes on one side; turn and cook another 4 minutes or until golden brown.

Sauteed Escarole and Cherry Tomatoes

1½   *teaspoons salt, divided*
2   *heads (about 2 pounds)*
       escarole, shredded
⅓   *cup olive oil*
1½   *tablespoons minced garlic*
¼   *teaspoon pepper*
1   *pint cherry tomatoes*

In large saucepot bring 1 inch water and 1 teaspoon salt to a boil. Add escarole and blanch 2 minutes; drain thoroughly.

Meanwhile, in large skillet heat oil over medium heat. Add garlic, remaining salt and pepper. Saute until garlic is golden; add tomatoes and cook, stirring occasionally, about 5 minutes. Transfer tomatoes to serving dish. To same skillet add escarole and cook, stirring constantly, about 1 minute. Combine escarole with tomatoes.

Strawberry Mousse

2   *packages (10 oz. each) frozen*
       quick-thaw strawberries
3   *teaspoons lemon juice*
2   *cups heavy or whipping*
       cream

Combine all ingredients in blender or food processor. Cover and blend or process until smooth and slightly thickened. Pour into 6 serving dishes and freeze until ready to serve, at least 15 minutes.

CHILLED CHERRY TOMATO APPETIZERS

For a festive first course, slice off tops of cherry tomatoes, gently squeeze out seeds and pulp, and stuff with:
* *smoked oysters and dash of lemon juice*
* *guacamole*
* *tuna, mayo, Dijon mustard and a grinding of fresh black pepper*

Steak Diane

FILET MIGNON FLAMED WITH BRANDY

Steak Diane, with its cognac and lemon sauce, is a classic company entree. We've surrounded it with hearty potatoes and a salad—quick, satisfying and elegant.

Menu for 6

- **Steak Diane**
  Dinner-Style
  Fried Potatoes
  Tossed Salad
  with

- **Blue Cheese**
  Dressing
  Napoleons

SHOPPING LIST

- ☐ 6   filets mignons, ¾ inch thick (about 1½ pounds)
- ☐   Salad greens
- ☐ 1   bunch fresh parsley
- ☐ 4   napoleons
- ☐ 1   8-ounce container sour cream
- ☐ ¼   pound blue cheese
- ☐ 1   24-ounce package frozen dinner-style fried potatoes

Have on Hand
- ☐   Salt
- ☐   Pepper
- ☐   Chives
- ☐ 1   lemon or lemon juice
- ☐   Vinegar

- ☐   Mayonnaise
- ☐   Worcestershire sauce
- ☐   Milk
- ☐   Butter
- ☐   Cognac

SCHEDULE

1. Prepare tossed salad and Blue Cheese Dressing; refrigerate separately.
2. Cook frozen dinner-style fried potatoes according to package directions.
3. Prepare Steak Diane.

Steak Diane

6	tablespoons butter, divided
6	filets mignons, ¾ inch thick (about 1½ pounds)
3	tablespoons cognac
1½	teaspoons lemon juice
1½	teaspoons Worcestershire sauce
¼	teaspoon pepper
2	tablespoons chopped chives
2	tablespoons chopped parsley

In heavy skillet melt 3 tablespoons butter over low heat. Increase heat to high. When foam subsides, add steaks and brown quickly on both sides. Cook 6 minutes total for rare, 8 minutes for medium.

In small saucepan warm cognac. Light with long-handled match and pour over steaks. When flame dies out, transfer steaks to serving platter. Add lemon juice, Worcestershire sauce, pepper and chives to skillet; heat through. Add remaining 3 tablespoons butter and stir just until melted. Pour sauce over steaks. Sprinkle with parsley.

Blue Cheese Dressing

⅔	cup sour cream
⅓	cup mayonnaise
1	tablespoon milk
½	cup crumbled blue cheese
1	tablespoon vinegar
	Dash salt
	Dash pepper

In small bowl combine all ingredients. Toss with greens just before serving.

STEAK TIPS

For special occasions you'll want to splurge on filet mignon, the choicest cut of steak, which comes from the eye of the tenderloin. Almost as succulent and delicious, however, are several other cuts:

- *Top loin steaks, sometimes called Kansas City steaks or New York strip steaks, are tender and juicy; broil or pan-broil them, being extra careful not to dry them out by overcooking.*
- *Rib eye steaks, an excellent choice for broiling, should be thick, and rare or medium rare.*
- *Sirloin and T-bone, also tender and tasty, are fine for pan-frying or broiling.*
- *Shell steaks, smaller and usually cut thinner than the others, can be broiled or pan-fried; look for supermarket specials on these.*

Swordfish Steaks

LIGHT ELEGANCE WITH BROILED FISH

From the quick-and-easy pâté to the creamy Camembert and cool grapes, this light meal makes an elegant and stylish statement. Salmon steaks will do in place of swordfish, Brie in place of Camembert, depending on season and availability.

Menu for 6

- **Chutney Pâté**
  Water Biscuits
- **Horseradish**
  Green Bean
  Salad
  French Bread

Broiled Swordfish
Steaks with
Lemon Wedges
Camembert
Cheese and
Green Grapes

SHOPPING LIST

- ☐ 6 swordfish steaks (about ½ pound each)
- ☐ ½ pound liverwurst
- ☐ 1½ pounds fresh green beans
- ☐ 1 medium onion
- ☐ 1½ pounds green grapes
- ☐ 1 small jar mango chutney
- ☐ 1 package water biscuits
- ☐ 1 loaf crusty French bread
- ☐ 1 4- or 5½-ounce Camembert cheese

Have on Hand

- ☐ Bacon
- ☐ Salt
- ☐ Pepper
- ☐ 1 lemon or lemon juice
- ☐ Mayonnaise
- ☐ Butter or margarine
- ☐ Worcestershire sauce
- ☐ Horseradish

SCHEDULE

1. Set Camembert out to come to room temperature.
2. Cook green beans and bacon; prepare horseradish dressing.
3. Prepare Chutney Pâté.
4. Broil swordfish steaks.

Chutney Pâté

½ pound liverwurst
½ cup butter, softened
¼ cup mango chutney
1   tablespoon horseradish

In small mixer bowl beat liverwurst with butter, chutney and horseradish until smooth. Scoop into dish and serve with water biscuits.

Horseradish Green Bean Salad

1½ pounds fresh whole green
*   beans, trimmed*
½   teaspoon salt
¾   cup mayonnaise
1   tablespoon horseradish
1   teaspoon Worcestershire
*   sauce*
*   Dash pepper*
*   Juice of 1 lemon*
1   medium onion, thinly
*   sliced*
3   slices bacon, cooked and
*   crumbled*

In medium saucepan cook beans in 1 inch salted water just until tender-crisp. Drain and plunge into cold water to cool. Cover and refrigerate.

In 1-cup measure blend mayonnaise with horseradish, Worcestershire sauce, pepper and lemon juice. In large bowl toss green beans with onion slices and crumbled bacon. Just before serving, add dressing and toss again.

HORSERADISH TIPS

- *Horseradish is a root with a strong, peppery flavor—an excellent accompaniment to many foods.*
- *Freshly prepared horseradish is especially pungent and tangy, and very easy to make if you have a blender or food processor. Scrub the horseradish root and peel off the outer skin. Cut into pieces and grate in the blender or process with the steel blade. For each cup of grated horseradish root add ½ cup distilled white vinegar or white wine vinegar, and ¼ teaspoon salt, if desired. For "red" horseradish, add a little grated beet. Store in the refrigerator in a jar with a tight-fitting lid.*
- *For flavor and zip, add a nip of horseradish:*
- *to Bloody Marys*
- *to shrimp cocktail sauce*
- *to prepared mustard, for extra tang*
- *to butter for corn on the cob*
- *to whipped or sour cream as an accompaniment to roast beef, smoked salmon or tongue*
- *to pickle relish for hot dogs*
- *to cole slaw dressing*
- *to cream cheese for a cracker spread*

Chicken Jubilee

CHERRIES AND CHICKEN—CAUSE FOR JUBILATION

Accompanied by carrot-studded orzo and tender-crisp steamed asparagus, this chicken entree is a variation of the classic Cherries Jubilee. We think you'll love our unusual dessert variation on the ever-popular Irish Coffee.

Menu for 6

- **Chicken Jubilee**
- **Orzo with Shredded Carrots**
- **Steamed Asparagus**
- **Irish Coffee Sundaes**

SHOPPING LIST

- ☐ 6 chicken cutlets
- ☐ 2 pounds fresh asparagus
- ☐ 1 pound carrots
- ☐ 1 8¾-ounce can dark sweet pitted cherries in juice
- ☐ 1 16-ounce package orzo (rice-shaped pasta)
- ☐ ½ pint heavy cream
- ☐ 1 quart coffee ice cream
- ☐ Irish cream liqueur
- ☐ Coffee bean candies (optional)

Have on Hand

- ☐ All-purpose flour
- ☐ Salt
- ☐ Pepper
- ☐ Butter or margarine
- ☐ Red currant jelly
- ☐ Brandy

SCHEDULE

1. Cook Orzo with Shredded Carrots.
2. Prepare steamed asparagus.
3. Prepare Chicken Jubilee.
4. Prepare Irish Coffee Sundaes.

Chicken Jubilee

½   cup flour
1   teaspoon salt
¼   teaspoon pepper
6   chicken cutlets
3   tablespoons butter or
        margarine
1   can (8¾-oz.) dark, sweet
        pitted cherries in juice
1   tablespoon red currant
        jelly
3   tablespoons brandy

Combine flour, salt and pepper in paper or plastic bag; shake chicken to coat. In heavy skillet heat butter or margarine; add chicken and brown 5 minutes on each side. Add cherries with juice, currant jelly and brandy. Boil 1 minute.

Orzo with Shredded Carrots

2   cups orzo
½   teaspoon salt
½   cup shredded carrot

Cook orzo in salted water according to package directions; drain well. Transfer to serving dish and toss with shredded carrot.

Irish Coffee Sundaes

1   quart coffee ice cream
¾   cup Irish cream liqueur
½   cup heavy cream, whipped
        Coffee bean candies
        (optional)

Place 1 scoop of ice cream in each dish. Top each with 2 tablespoons liqueur and a dollop of whipped cream. Garnish with candies, if desired.

STEAMED ASPARAGUS

In a steamer or large saucepan with a rack, heat ½ inch water to boiling. Add 1 to 2 pounds asparagus, tied in a bundle. Cover and steam 8 to 10 minutes, until tender-crisp. To serve steamed asparagus:

- *Toss with chopped pimiento*
- *Top with oven-toasted pine nuts or sliced almonds*
- *Garnish with lemon wedges*
- *Toss with sliced green onions*
- *Serve with 3 tablespoons melted butter mixed with 1 tablespoon snipped fresh dill*
- *Garnish with broiled tomato wedges or trimmed cherry tomatoes*
- *Top with toasted bread crumbs or garlic-flavored croutons*
- *Top with hollandaise sauce— fresh, bottled or made from a mix*
- *Toss with chopped water chestnuts*

Spaghetti Carbonara
QUICK ITALIAN FEAST FOR SURPRISE VISITORS

This Mediterranean menu with its unusual appetizer will be a hit with guests of all ages. Everything in this meal is Italian, right down to the arugula in the salad. No arugula in your market? Try radicchio instead. In a pinch, spinach is also a good substitute.

Menu for 6

- **Zucchini Pizzas**
- **Spaghetti Carbonara Breadsticks**

- **Arugula and Romaine Salad**
- **Fresh Fruit with Marsala**

SHOPPING LIST

- ☐ 1 pound bacon
- ☐ 1 pound thin spaghetti
- ☐ 2 bunches green onions
- ☐ 1 large zucchini
- ☐ 1 head arugula
- ☐ 1 head romaine lettuce
- ☐ 1 pint strawberries
- ☐ 2 bananas
- ☐ 2 oranges
- ☐ 1 jar pizza sauce
- ☐ 1 small can ripe olives
- ☐ 1 package breadsticks
- ☐ 8 ounces shredded Cheddar cheese
- ☐ 6 ounces mozzarella

Have on Hand
- ☐ Sugar
- ☐ Salt
- ☐ Pepper
- ☐ Eggs
- ☐ Butter or margarine
- ☐ Salad dressing
- ☐ Vanilla extract
- ☐ Sweet Marsala wine

SCHEDULE

1. Cook spaghetti.
2. Prepare Zucchini Pizzas.
3. Assemble salad.
4. Prepare dessert.
5. Prepare Spaghetti Carbonara.

Zucchini Pizzas

1   large zucchini, cut into
      *¹/₄-inch slices (about
      24 slices)*
      Salt
1¹/₂ *cups pizza sauce*
¹/₂ *cup chopped ripe olives*
¹/₂ *cup minced green onion*
1¹/₂ *cups (6 oz.) shredded
      mozzarella, Monterey
      Jack or other white
      cheese*

Preheat broiler. Salt zucchini lightly. Place slices on cookie sheet and top each with 1 tablespoon pizza sauce, 1 teaspoon olives, 1 teaspoon green onion and 1 tablespoon cheese. Broil 5 inches from heat until cheese is melted and bubbly, 4 to 5 minutes.

Spaghetti Carbonara

1   *pound thin spaghetti*
¹/₂ *pound bacon, cut in 1-inch
      pieces*
1   *cup chopped green onions*
¹/₂ *cup butter or margarine*
2   *cups (8 oz.) shredded
      Cheddar cheese*
¹/₄ *teaspoon salt*
¹/₈ *teaspoon pepper*
4   *eggs, lightly beaten*

Cook spaghetti according to package directions. Drain; keep warm.

In large skillet cook bacon until crisp. Drain on paper towels, reserving 2 tablespoons drippings in skillet. Add green onions and mushrooms; saute over low heat 2 minutes.

In same skillet melt butter or margarine. Add spaghetti, bacon, cheese and seasonings; toss lightly to combine. Add eggs gradually and mix well. Remove from heat. Toss and serve immediately.

Fresh Fruit with Marsala

2   *tablespoons sugar*
¹/₄ *cup sweet Marsala wine*
1   *pint strawberries*
2   *medium bananas*
2   *oranges, peeled and sliced*

In medium bowl combine sugar and Marsala; stir until sugar is dissolved. Add fruit and toss. Spoon into dessert dishes.

TASTY ZUCCHINI APPETIZER

Simmer 6 small whole zucchini in water to cover about 7 minutes, until just tender. Plunge into cold water until cool enough to handle. Halve the zucchini lengthwise and sprinkle cut sides with Italian-flavored bread crumbs or grated Parmesan cheese. Bake in 450°F. oven until heated through.

Orange Beef

A TEN-MINUTE ENTREE

Here is a perfect menu for an impromptu summer dinner. The entree is an interesting alternative to ordinary broiled or barbecued beef. You'll want to use this broccoli recipe for family meals too, and these rich, summery Peach Smoothies are sure to delight your guests.

Menu for 6

- **Orange Beef**
  Steamed Rice
- **Mandarin-Style**
  Broccoli

Radishes and
Green Onions
- **Peach**
  Smoothies

SHOPPING LIST

- ☐ 1½ pounds beef cube steak
- ☐ 1 bunch broccoli
- ☐ 1 bunch radishes
- ☐ 1 bunch green onions
- ☐ 1 orange
- ☐ 1 16-ounce can peaches in heavy syrup
- ☐ 1 8-ounce package cream cheese
- ☐ 1 8-ounce container sour cream

Have on Hand

- ☐ Long-grain rice
- ☐ Cornstarch
- ☐ Salt
- ☐ Garlic

- ☐ Crushed red pepper
- ☐ Ginger
- ☐ Olive oil
- ☐ Salad oil
- ☐ Soy sauce
- ☐ Dark rum

SCHEDULE

1. Prepare Peach Smoothies.
2. Cook rice.
3. Clean and trim radishes and green onions.
4. Prepare Orange Beef.
5. Cook Mandarin-Style Broccoli.

Orange Beef

1   orange
1½ pounds beef cube steaks
3   tablespoons cornstarch
2   tablespoons salad oil
1   garlic clove, crushed
½   teaspoon ground ginger
2   tablespoons soy sauce

Grate orange peel. Squeeze orange; set peel and juice aside. Cut steak into ½-inch-wide strips; dredge in cornstarch. In large skillet heat oil. Add meat, grated orange peel, garlic and ginger. Stir-fry 3 to 4 minutes; transfer to serving plate. Add orange juice and soy sauce to skillet; bring to a boil. Pour sauce over beef.

Mandarin-Style Broccoli

2   tablespoons vegetable oil
2   tablespoons olive oil
¼   teaspoon crushed red
      pepper
1   bunch broccoli, trimmed
      and cut into pieces
¼   teaspoon salt

In heavy skillet or wok heat oils. Add red pepper and broccoli; stir-fry 3 minutes. Cover and cook over medium heat 4 to 6 minutes or until broccoli is tender but still crisp. Sprinkle with salt.

Peach Smoothies

1   package (8 oz.) cream
      cheese
1   can (16 oz.) peaches in
      heavy syrup
1   tablespoon dark rum
1   cup sour cream

Cut cream cheese into chunks and put into blender. Drain peaches, reserving 5 tablespoons syrup. Add fruit, reserved syrup and rum to blender; blend until smooth. Stir in sour cream. Pour into 6 dessert dishes; chill in freezer 25 minutes.

INSTANT ZEST WITH ORANGE FLAVOR

- *Stir a can of orange juice concentrate into 1 quart softened vanilla ice cream; refreeze until firm.*
- *Spoon over sauteed ham slice during last minutes of cooking.*
- *To each acorn squash half, add 1 teaspoon orange juice concentrate, 1 teaspoon butter and a sprinkle of cinnamon before baking.*

Broiled Garlic Lamb Chops

ON-THE-RUN LAMB CHOP DINNER

These chops marinate while you prepare the rest of the meal (or overnight, if that suits your schedule better). Add flavor to the tiny pasta with green onions and sharp feta cheese.

═══ Menu for 6 ═══

- **Broiled Garlicky Lamb Chops**
- **Orzo with Feta and Green Onions**
- **Sliced Tomatoes and Cucumbers with Ripe Olives**
- **Oil and Vinegar Dressing**
- **Coffee Frappés**

SHOPPING LIST

- ☐ 6   shoulder lamb chops, 1 inch thick
- ☐ 1   16-ounce package orzo (rice-shaped pasta)
- ☐ 1   bunch green onions
- ☐ 1   bunch fresh parsley
- ☐ 2   or 3 tomatoes
- ☐ 2   medium cucumbers
- ☐ 1   small can ripe olives
- ☐ 2   ounces feta cheese
- ☐ 1/2   pint heavy or whipping cream
- ☐ 1   quart coffee ice cream
- ☐   Crème de cacao

Have on Hand
- ☐   Salt
- ☐   Pepper
- ☐   Garlic
- ☐   Oregano
- ☐   Butter or margarine
- ☐   Salad oil
- ☐   Vinegar
- ☐   Dry red wine
- ☐   Brandy

SCHEDULE

1. Mix marinade; add chops and marinate.
2. Cook orzo.
3. Prepare salad.
4. Whip cream for dessert.
5. Broil chops.

Broiled Garlicky Lamb Chops

6   shoulder lamb chops,
      1 inch thick
1   cup dry red wine
1/3 cup salad oil
2   garlic cloves, crushed
1   teaspoon oregano, crushed
1/2 teaspoon salt
1/4 teaspoon pepper

Arrange chops in large baking dish. In 2-cup measure combine remaining ingredients and pour over chops, turning to coat. Cover and marinate 15 minutes or longer.

Preheat broiler. Drain chops; pat dry. Broil 3 inches from heat about 4 minutes on each side for rare, 5 to 6 minutes for medium.

Orzo with Feta and Green Onions

      Water
2   cups orzo (rice-shaped
      pasta)
1 1/2 teaspoons salt
3   tablespoons butter or
      margarine
2   large green onions, sliced
1/2 cup (2 oz.) finely
      crumbled feta cheese
2   tablespoons chopped
      parsley
      Dash pepper

In 4-quart saucepot bring water to a boil. Add orzo and salt. Boil, stirring occasionally, until tender, 10 to 12 minutes. Drain. In medium skillet melt butter or margarine. Add green onions; saute over medium heat 3 minutes. Stir in orzo, feta, parsley and pepper.

Coffee Frappés

3   tablespoons creme de cacao
3   tablespoons brandy
1   quart coffee ice cream
1/2 cup heavy or whipping
      cream, whipped

Combine creme de cacao, brandy and ice cream in blender. Cover and whirl until smooth and foamy. Pour into serving glasses or brandy snifters. Garnish with whipped cream.

LAMB CHOP TIPS

• *In shopping for lamb, look for bones that are spongy and red in the center.*
• *Flesh of top-quality lamb will be moist, evenly dark red and faintly marbled.*
• *To saute lamb chops, heat butter or oil in large skillet. Add chops and cook 3 to 5 minutes on each side for rare to medium rare.*

Trout Amandine

FRESH FILLETS SAUTEED WITH ALMONDS

Sauteed almonds add crunch and flavor to this deli-cate trout entree. Serve it with creamed potatoes like the ones that Mother used to make.

Menu for 6

- **Trout Amandine**
- **Creamed New Potatoes and Peas**

Broiled Tomato Halves with Parsley

Ambrosia

SHOPPING LIST

- ☐ 6 trout fillets or other fresh white fish fillets
- ☐ 1 bunch parsley
- ☐ 1½ pounds small new potatoes
- ☐ 6 tomatoes
- ☐ 3 oranges
- ☐ 2 lemons
- ☐ 3 bananas
- ☐ 1 13¾- or 14½-ounce can chicken broth
- ☐ 1 small can or package shredded coconut
- ☐ 1 small package chopped or slivered almonds
- ☐ 1 small can or package whole pecans
- ☐ ½ pint heavy or whipping cream
- ☐ 1 10-ounce package frozen peas

Have on Hand
- ☐ All-purpose flour
- ☐ Salt
- ☐ Pepper
- ☐ Sugar
- ☐ Milk
- ☐ Butter or margarine
- ☐ Dry white wine

SCHEDULE

1. Prepare Creamed New Potatoes and Peas.
2. Prepare Ambrosia.
3. Cook Trout Amandine.
4. Prepare Broiled Tomato Halves.

Trout Amandine

1/3   cup butter or margarine
1/2   cup chopped or slivered
     almonds
1   cup milk
1/2   cup all-purpose flour
1/4   teaspoon salt
1/8   teaspoon pepper
6   trout fillets or other fresh
     white fish fillets
1/3   cup dry white wine
     Parsley
2   lemons, cut into wedges

In large skillet melt butter or margarine. Add almonds; saute until lightly browned. Remove with slotted spoon and set aside.

Pour milk into shallow dish. In another shallow dish combine flour with salt and pepper. Dip trout fillets first in milk, then in flour. In drippings in same skillet cook trout on both sides over medium-high heat until lightly browned. Add wine; heat to boiling. Transfer to serving dish. Sprinkle almonds over fish. Garnish with parsley and lemon wedges.

Creamed New Potatoes and Peas

1 1/2   pounds small new
      potatoes, unpeeled
1 1/2   teaspoons salt, divided
1/4   cup butter or margarine
1/4   cup all-purpose flour
3/4   cup chicken broth
1 1/2   cups milk

1/8   teaspoon pepper
1   package (10 oz.) frozen
     peas, cooked and
     drained
2   tablespoons chopped
     parsley

In large saucepan combine potatoes and 1 teaspoon salt. Add water to cover and bring to a boil over high heat. Cook until fork-tender, 15 to 20 minutes. Drain and keep warm.

In medium saucepan melt butter or margarine over low heat. Stir in flour and whisk until smooth. Cook 2 to 3 minutes, stirring occasionally. Gradually stir in chicken broth, milk, remaining 1/2 teaspoon salt and pepper. Cook over medium heat until thick and smooth, stirring frequently, about 5 minutes. Add peas and parsley; heat through. Spoon potatoes into a serving dish and top with peas and sauce.

START WITH A PACKAGE OF FROZEN PEAS . . .

- *Add sliced mushrooms, chopped celery and cook.*
- *To cooked peas add diced pimiento and sliced ripe olive.*
- *Prepare macaroni and cheese; add cooked frankfurters and peas.*
- *Thaw peas but do not cook; toss with sour cream, chopped green onions and crumbled bacon.*
- *Cook peas with a package of frozen cauliflower in cream sauce.*

Entertaining Tips

Little Things to See To Before the Doorbell Rings

- *Post schedule of menu and recipes on refrigerator door or kitchen bulletin board. Many a hostess in the rush of serving has forgotten the warming rolls or the special sauce for the dessert.*
- *Polish and fill salt and pepper shakers. Replenish sugar bowl.*
- *Dust off the telephone, books, records, picture frames.*
- *Remove dead leaves from plants.*
- *Clear away fragile or valuable objects.*
- *Set fresh towels out in the bathroom. Make sure there's plenty of toilet tissue. Be sure all bathrooms are tidy; guests have a way of wandering.*
- *Get rid of garbage and old newspapers.*
- *Close (and lock) doors to off-limit rooms.*
- *Settle pets comfortably out of party range or ask a neighbor to "pet-sit."*
- *Open windows, if only for ten minutes, to freshen air.*

To Insure a Successful Brunch:

- *Ask guests to gather around noon.*
- *Plan to serve food by one o'clock—to cut hunger pangs or over-imbibing.*
- *Serve just two kinds of drinks (plus one for teetotalers) to avoid being a slave to cocktail orders. Make batches in advance.*
- *Spiff up your brunch with country-style tablecloth and napkins (or use inexpensive bandannas), sturdy goblets for drinks.*
- *Serve the best coffee—freshly brewed, dark and aromatic. Try experimenting with espresso, cappuccino or, for a warm glow, Irish Coffee topped with whipped cream.*

Quick Cream Cheese Snacks

- Tea-Time Spread: *Unwrap a package of cream cheese, top with mango chutney and sprinkle with toasted slivered almonds. Pass with crackers. This snack also goes well with cold drinks or cocktails.*

- Blue Cheese Spread: *Soften cream cheese and blue cheese. Blend to taste and serve with crackers, accompanied by seedless grapes.*

Quickies with Leftovers

- *When cooking a fish dish, make more than you need—intentionally. Chill leftovers and de-bone (if necessary). Mix with mayonnaise and chopped celery; use in place of tuna for sandwiches—it's a nice change.*

- *Grind leftover cooked meat, toss with onion, chopped dill pickle and prepared mustard for a deviled sandwich spread.*

How to Carve Carrot Blossoms

Start with a chunky—not long and tapered—carrot; peel and remove top so you start with a flat end. Cut out five or six lengthwise, V-shaped wedges. Then cut into ¼-inch crosswise slices. Perfect as a pretty garnish for salads or main courses or an interesting, fun way to serve an everyday cooked vegetable.

Carve a Radish Rose

Cut off root and stem ends of radish. With sharp knife, make two criss-cross indentations on radish top, forming a star pattern. Create petals by slicing down on each side just to the bottom, being careful not to cut through. Drop into ice water to allow the petals to open.

Turkey with Cumin Sauce, page 36

Veal with Mushroom Sauce, page 38

Turkey with Cumin Sauce

A FLAVORFUL MAIN DISH

A highly spiced tomato sauce enlivens turkey (or chicken) cutlets for a dish easy on your budget as well as your schedule. Team it with sauteed zucchini and sesame bread, and follow with cool and luscious Mint Dreams dessert.

Menu for 6

- **Turkey with Cumin Sauce**
- **Herbed Zucchini**
- **Sesame Seed Bread**
- **Mint Dreams**

SHOPPING LIST

- ☐ 6 turkey cutlets
- ☐ 1 bunch green onions
- ☐ 3 medium zucchini
- ☐ 2 16-ounce cans whole tomatoes
- ☐ 1 loaf sesame seed bread
- ☐ ½ pint heavy or whipping cream
- ☐ 1 quart mint chocolate chip ice cream
- ☐ Green or white crème de menthe

Have on Hand
- ☐ Sugar

- ☐ Salt
- ☐ Pepper
- ☐ Cumin
- ☐ Garlic
- ☐ Chives
- ☐ Salad oil
- ☐ Butter or margarine

SCHEDULE

1. Prepare Turkey with Cumin Sauce.
2. Cook Herbed Zucchini.
3. Prepare Mint Dreams.

Turkey with Cumin Sauce

2 cans (16 oz. each) whole
   tomatoes
6 turkey cutlets
½ teaspoon salt, divided
¼ teaspoon pepper, divided
2 tablespoons salad oil
2 small garlic cloves,
   crushed
2 teaspoons cumin
1 cup water
½ teaspoon sugar
¼ cup chopped green onions

Drain and chop tomatoes, reserving 1 cup juice for sauce; set aside. Place cutlets between 2 sheets wax paper. Pound to ¼-inch thickness. Sprinkle with ¼ teaspoon salt and ⅛ teaspoon pepper.

In heavy skillet heat oil over medium-high heat. Add cutlets and cook 2 minutes on each side. Remove from skillet, cover and set aside. Saute garlic and cumin in drippings 30 seconds. Add tomatoes, reserved juice, water, sugar and remaining salt and pepper. Cook over high heat 10 minutes, stirring occasionally. Reduce heat and add cutlets to sauce. Simmer 2 minutes, spooning sauce over cutlets. Garnish with green onions.

Herbed Zucchini

2 tablespoons salad oil
3 medium zucchini, cut into
   ¼-inch slices
1 tablespoon chopped chives
½ teaspoon salt
⅛ teaspoon pepper
1 tablespoon butter or
   margarine

In a large skillet heat oil. Add zucchini in a single layer; saute over high heat for 5 minutes. Add chives, salt, pepper and butter or margarine and toss well.

Mint Dreams

1 cup heavy or whipping
   cream
4 tablespoons white or green
   crème de menthe
1 quart mint chocolate chip
   ice cream

Whip the cream until soft peaks form. Blend in crème de menthe. Place 1 or 2 scoops ice cream in each dessert dish. Top each serving with a dollop of mint whipped cream.

QUICK DESSERTS WITH CRÈME DE MENTHE

- *Splash green crème de menthe over scoops of vanilla or vanilla chocolate chip ice cream.*
- *Splash white crème de menthe over chocolate or chocolate chocolate chip ice cream.*

Veal Cutlets with Mushroom Sauce

EASY ELEGANCE FOR ENJOYABLE ENTERTAINING

Here is an extra-special meal for your very important guests. Serve fresh Asparagus Vinaigrette if that much-favored vegetable is in season; if not, frozen will do very well.

Menu for 6

- **Asparagus Vinaigrette**
- **Veal Cutlets with Mushroom Sauce**
  Rice with Parsley
- **Dilled Carrots**
  Coffee Ice Cream with Coffee Liqueur and Walnuts

SHOPPING LIST

- ☐ 2 pounds veal cutlets
- ☐ 1½ pounds fresh asparagus spears or 2 10-ounce packages frozen
- ☐ 1 pound carrots
- ☐ 1 onion
- ☐ 3 large shallots
- ☐ ¾ pound mushrooms
- ☐ 1 bunch fresh parsley
- ☐ 1 bunch fresh dill or dillweed
- ☐ 2 lemons
- ☐ 1 small can or package walnuts
- ☐ 1 pint heavy or whipping cream
- ☐ 1 quart coffee ice cream

Have on Hand
- ☐ Long-grain rice

- ☐ Salt
- ☐ Pepper
- ☐ Garlic powder
- ☐ Onion salt
- ☐ Salad oil
- ☐ Butter or margarine
- ☐ Coffee liqueur

SCHEDULE

1. Cook asparagus and chill.
2. Cook rice.
3. Prepare Veal with Mushroom Sauce.
4. Cook Carrots.
5. Prepare Asparagus Vinaigrette.

Asparagus Vinaigrette

1½ **pound fresh asparagus spears, trimmed or 2 packages (10 oz. each) frozen**
4 **tablespoons salad oil**
2 **tablespoons lemon juice**
   Dash garlic powder
   Dash onion salt
   Grated lemon rind
   Lemon slices

In saucepan cook asparagus in water to cover for 8 to 10 minutes until just tender-crisp. (Cook frozen asparagus according to package directions.) Drain and chill. In small bowl combine oil, lemon juice, garlic powder and onion salt. Just before serving, pour dressing over asparagus. Garnish with grated lemon rind and lemon slices.

Veal Cutlets with Mushroom Sauce

3 **tablespoons butter or margarine**
⅓ **cup minced shallots**
¾ **pound mushrooms, sliced**
½ **teaspoon salt, divided**
   Dash pepper
2 **cups heavy or whipping cream**
2 **pounds veal cutlets, pounded thin**
½ **cup all-purpose flour**
4 **tablespoons salad oil**

In heavy skillet melt butter or margarine over medium heat. Add shallots, mushrooms, ¼ teaspoon salt and dash pepper.

Cook, stirring occasionally, until all liquid evaporates and mushrooms begin to brown, 10 to 12 minutes. Pour in cream. Bring to a boil; reduce heat and simmer until sauce is reduced to about 2¼ cups, about 10 minutes.

In pie plate or on platter dredge veal cutlets in flour seasoned with ¼ teaspoon salt and dash pepper. In another heavy skillet heat oil. Saute cutlets about 2 minutes on each side, until cooked through but not brown. Serve with mushroom sauce.

Dilled Carrots

2 **tablespoons butter or margarine**
1 **medium onion, chopped**
1 **large bunch carrots, thinly sliced**
¼ **cup water**
2 **teaspoons chopped fresh dill or ¾ teaspoon dillweed**
¼ **teaspoon salt**

In large skillet melt butter or margarine over medium heat. Add onion and saute 2 minutes. Add carrots, water, dillweed and salt. Cook 5 minutes, stirring occasionally. Reduce heat to low, cover and cook 10 minutes or until carrots are tender.

BUYING FRESH ASPARAGUS

Look for asparagus with straight stalks of uniform thickness with closed, compact tips and a good green color.

Chicken Veronique, page 42

Chocolate Love, page 44

Barbecued Steak, page 46

Caviar Appetizer, page 48

Veal Piccata, page 50

Chicken Veronique

SAUCY FRENCH CHICKEN WITH GRAPES

A zesty sauce made with mandarin oranges and grapes gives this delectable chicken dish four-star flavor. Dress up the rice with the spicy fragrance and flavor of ground cloves, and add vitamins and color with a salad of spinach and bean sprouts.

Menu for 6

- **Chicken Veronique**
- **Clove-Seasoned Rice**
- **Spinach and Bean Sprout Salad**
- **Butterscotch Parfaits**

SHOPPING LIST

- ☐ 6 chicken cutlets
- ☐ ¼ pound bean sprouts
- ☐ 1 bunch seedless green grapes
- ☐ 1 11-ounce can mandarin oranges
- ☐ 1 small jar butterscotch topping
- ☐ 1 small box granola
- ☐ 1 10-ounce package fresh spinach
- ☐ 1 quart vanilla ice cream

Have on Hand

- ☐ Long-grain rice
- ☐ Cornstarch
- ☐ Salt
- ☐ Pepper
- ☐ Dry mustard
- ☐ Ground cloves
- ☐ Orange marmalade
- ☐ 1 lemon or lemon juice
- ☐ Salad dressing
- ☐ Butter or margarine

SCHEDULE

1. Cook Clove-Seasoned Rice.
2. Prepare Chicken Veronique.
3. Assemble salad.
4. Prepare Butterscotch Parfaits.

Chicken Veronique

6   chicken cutlets
¾   teaspoon salt
¼   teaspoon pepper
2   tablespoons butter or
        margarine
½   cup orange marmalade
1   tablespoon cornstarch
1   tablespoon lemon juice
½   teaspoon dry mustard
1   can (11 oz.) mandarin
        oranges, drained
1   cup fresh seedless green
        grapes

Sprinkle chicken cutlets with salt and pepper. In large skillet melt butter over medium heat. Add chicken and brown on both sides about 10 minutes. In small bowl combine orange marmalade, cornstarch, lemon juice and dry mustard. Fold in mandarin oranges and grapes. Pour sauce over chicken; cover and simmer 15 minutes.

Clove-Seasoned Rice

3   cups water
3   tablespoons butter or
        margarine
½   teaspoon salt
¼   teaspoon ground
        cloves
1½   cups long-grain rice

In medium saucepan combine water with butter or margarine, salt and ground cloves. Heat to boiling. Add rice and stir. Cover and simmer 20 minutes or until rice is tender and water is absorbed.

Butterscotch Parfaits

1   quart vanilla ice cream
¾   cup butterscotch topping
¼   cup granola

In each of six parfait glasses place a small scoop of ice cream, then 1 tablespoon butterscotch topping and 2 teaspoons granola. Repeat; top with granola.

QUICK CRUNCH WITH BEAN SPROUTS

Leftover sprouts from your Spinach and Bean Sprout Salad?
* *Top baked potatoes with sour cream and a sprinkling of sprouts.*
* *Toss some into bacon, lettuce and tomato sandwiches.*
* *Add to scrambled eggs and shredded Cheddar cheese; serve in toasted pita breads for lunch or breakfast.*

Linguine with Spinach-Walnut Sauce

ITALIAN MENU ON THE LIGHT SIDE

This linguine entree—tossed with a blender puree of fresh spinach and walnuts—is a refreshing change from pasta with meat and tomato sauce.

Menu for 6

- **Antipasto**
- **Linguine with Spinach-Walnut Sauce**

Chicory and Tomato Salad
Italian Bread
- **Chocolate Love**

SHOPPING LIST

- ☐ 12 thin slices Genoa salami
- ☐ 1 16-ounce package linguine
- ☐ 2 heads Bibb or Boston lettuce
- ☐ 1 10-ounce package fresh spinach
- ☐ 1 bunch fresh parsley
- ☐ 1 head chicory
- ☐ 2 tomatoes
- ☐ 2 pints fresh strawberries
- ☐ 1 7-ounce jar roasted red peppers
- ☐ 1 small can or jar ripe olives
- ☐ 1 small can or package chopped walnuts
- ☐ 1 12-ounce package semisweet chocolate chips
- ☐ 1 loaf Italian bread

- ☐ ½ pint heavy or whipping cream

Have on Hand
- ☐ Salt
- ☐ Olive or salad oil
- ☐ Garlic
- ☐ Italian salad dressing
- ☐ Grated Parmesan cheese
- ☐ Amaretto

SCHEDULE

1. Prepare salad.
2. Prepare Chocolate Love.
3. Cook linguine.
4. Arrange Antipasto.
5. Prepare Linguine with Spinach-Walnut Sauce.

Antipasto

2 **heads Bibb or Boston lettuce**
1 **jar (7 oz.) roasted red peppers**
12 **thin slices Genoa salami**
12 **ripe olives**
½ **cup bottled Italian salad dressing**

Line salad platter with lettuce leaves. Arrange red peppers, salami and olives on lettuce. Serve with dressing on the side.

Linguine with Spinach-Walnut Sauce

1 **pound linguine**
2½ **cups fresh spinach leaves**
3 **sprigs parsley**
½ **cup grated Parmesan cheese**
3 **garlic cloves, halved**
1 **teaspoon salt**
¼ **cup olive or salad oil**
¼ **cup hot water**
½ **cup chopped walnuts**

Cook linguine according to package directions. Combine spinach, parsley, Parmesan, garlic, salt, oil and hot water in blender container. Puree until smooth, stopping blender occasionally and scraping down sides with rubber spatula. Fold in walnuts. Toss sauce with well-drained cooked linguine.

Chocolate Love

1½ **cups semisweet chocolate chips**
¾ **cup heavy or whipping cream**
6 **tablespoons amaretto**
2 **pints whole fresh strawberries, washed and well drained**

In a heavy 1-quart saucepan combine chocolate chips and cream. Heat, stirring constantly, over medium-low heat just until chocolate is melted and mixture is smooth. Stir in amaretto. Pour into small individual dishes and set aside. Serve with fresh strawberries.

ANTIPASTO TIPS

A good antipasto (the word means "before the pasta") is an attractive arrangement of Italian foods whose flavors, colors and textures complement one another. In addition to roasted peppers, salami and olives, you might want to include one or several of the following: rolled-up prosciutto, chunks of provolone cheese, hard-cooked egg wedges, anchovies, caponata, tomato wedges, marinated artichoke hearts, tuna chunks.

Barbecued Steak

FUSS-FREE SUMMER OR WINTER DINNER

Whether cooked on a backyard grill or in your kitchen, this steak, with its vermouth-flavored sauce, will satisfy both the appetite and the palate.

Menu for 6

- **Guacamole with Tortilla Chips**
- **Barbecued Steak Parsley Potatoes**
- **Tossed Salad with Classic Dressing**
- **Fruit-topped Cheesecake**

SHOPPING LIST

- ☐ 1 boneless 2-pound top round beef steak, about 1½ inches thick
- ☐ 1 large head romaine lettuce
- ☐ 1 small head chicory or escarole
- ☐ 1 bunch fresh parsley
- ☐ 1 green pepper
- ☐ 1 small cucumber
- ☐ 1 onion
- ☐ 8 small shallots
- ☐ 2 ripe avocados
- ☐ 1 12-ounce jar salsa
- ☐ 1 package tortilla chips
- ☐ 1 fruit-topped cheesecake

Have on Hand
- ☐ Sugar

- ☐ Salt
- ☐ Pepper
- ☐ Garlic
- ☐ Butter or margarine
- ☐ Salad oil
- ☐ Olive oil
- ☐ Red wine vinegar
- ☐ 1 lemon or lemon juice
- ☐ Dry vermouth

SCHEDULE

1. Cook potatoes.
2. Prepare Guacamole.
3. Prepare Tossed Salad with Classic Dressing.
4. Prepare Barbecued Steak.

Guacamole with Tortilla Chips

2 ripe avocados, peeled and
    pitted
1/3 cup finely chopped onion
1/3 cup salsa
2 tablespoons lemon juice
3/4 teaspoon salt
    Tortilla chips

In large bowl mash avocados with potato masher. Add onion, salsa, lemon juice and salt and stir until blended. Serve with tortilla chips.

Barbecued Steak

1 boneless 2-pound top round
    beef steak, 1½ inches thick
1/4 cup butter or margarine
1 cup coarsely chopped
    shallots or onions
2 tablespoons chopped parsley
1/4 cup dry vermouth
1 teaspoon salt
1/4 teaspoon pepper

Preheat broiler or prepare outdoor grill for barbecuing. Trim excess fat from edges of steaks; slash remaining fat at 2-inch intervals to prevent curling. Grill or broil steak 4 inches from heat 3 to 4 minutes on each side for rare, 6 to 7 minutes for medium, 8 to 10 inches for well done.

In small skillet melt butter or margarine. Add shallots or onions and saute until tender, 3 to 5 minutes. Add parsley and vermouth; simmer 3 minutes. Add salt and pepper. Serve with steak.

Tossed Salad with Classic Dressing

3 tablespoons olive oil
3 tablespoons salad oil
2 tablespoons red wine
    vinegar
1 garlic clove, peeled and
    cut in half
1/4 teaspoon salt
1/8 teaspoon pepper
1/4 teaspoon sugar
1 large head romaine
    lettuce, torn into
    pieces
1 small head chicory or
    escarole, torn into pieces
1 green pepper, sliced
1 small cucumber, sliced

In small jar with tight-fitting lid combine oils, vinegar, garlic, salt, pepper and sugar. Place greens in large salad bowl; toss with dressing.

BERRY CHEESECAKE

Crush 1 cup fresh berries and cook with 1 cup water 2 minutes; strain. Mix together 4½ teaspoons cornstarch and about ½ cup sugar (depending on sweetness of berries). Stir into strained juice and bring to a boil, stirring constantly until glaze thickens. Set aside to cool before spooning over cheesecake. Decorate glazed cheesecake with whole berries, if desired.

Chicken with Sherry

FOR A FESTIVE EVENING

Flatter your guests by offering them tiny new potatoes topped with dollops of cool sour cream and garnished with caviar. Then move on to a sherry-flavored chicken entree and a medley of zucchini, mushrooms and onions. Finish with a luscious dessert.

Menu for 6

- **Caviar-Topped New Potatoes**
- **Chicken with Sherry Rice**
- **Fresh Zucchini Medley**
- **Pecan Pie with Whipped Cream**

SHOPPING LIST

- ☐ 6   chicken cutlets
- ☐ 6   to 8 medium zucchini
- ☐ 1   pound tiny new potatoes
- ☐ 3   shallots
- ☐ 1   bunch parsley
- ☐ ½   pound small fresh mushrooms
- ☐ 1   2-ounce jar black or red lumpfish caviar
- ☐ 1   pecan pie
- ☐ 1   16-ounce package frozen small onions
- ☐ 1   8-ounce container sour cream
- ☐ ½   pint heavy or whipping cream

Have on Hand

- ☐   Salt
- ☐   Pepper
- ☐   Butter or margarine
- ☐   Garlic
- ☐   Salad oil
- ☐   All-purpose flour
- ☐   Long-grain rice
- ☐   Dry sherry

SCHEDULE

1. Cook rice.
2. Whip cream; refrigerate.
3. Cook Chicken with Sherry; keep warm.
4. Prepare Caviar-Topped Potatoes.
5. Cook Fresh Zucchini Medley.

Caviar-Topped Potatoes

1   pound tiny new potatoes
1/2   teaspoon salt
1/8   teaspoon pepper
3   shallots, minced
1/2   cup sour cream
1   2-ounce jar black or red
     lumpfish caviar

In large saucepan cover potatoes with water. Bring to a boil, cover and cook about 20 minutes. Drain and plunge into ice water to cool. Halve potatoes and trim so that they will stand up. Scoop out a small hole from each half; sprinkle cavities with salt, pepper and minced shallots. Fill with sour cream and top with caviar.

Chicken with Sherry

3/4   cup all-purpose flour
1/2   garlic clove, minced
1   teaspoon salt
     Dash pepper
6   chicken cutlets, sliced
     crosswise into 1-inch
     pieces
1/4   cup butter or margarine
1/4   cup dry sherry
2   tablespoons chopped
     parsley

In plastic or paper bag combine flour, garlic, salt and pepper. Add chicken pieces a few at a time and shake until well coated. In large skillet saute chicken pieces in butter or margarine until golden brown. Add sherry; cover and simmer 5 to 7 minutes or until chicken is tender. Transfer to serving platter and garnish with parsley.

Fresh Zucchini Medley

2   cups frozen small onions
1/2   pound small fresh
     mushrooms
6   to 8 medium zucchini
1   garlic clove
1/4   cup salad oil
3/4   teaspoon salt
     Dash pepper

Set onions out to thaw. Carefully cut caps off mushrooms and wipe clean with damp cloth, reserving stems for another use. Cut ends off zucchini and slice.

In Dutch oven or heavy skillet, heat oil. Add zucchini, mushrooms and garlic. Sprinkle with salt and pepper. Cook 5 to 8 minutes, stirring quickly and frequently, until vegetables are tender-crisp. Add onions and cook about 5 minutes.

QUICK CAVIAR APPETIZER

- Red Caviar Dip: *Combine an 8-ounce container of sour cream with a 2-ounce jar of red caviar and 1 tablespoon minced onion; serve with raw vegetables.*

Veal Piccata

AN ELEGANT COMPANY DINNER

*This festive dinner, perfect for any occasion, features
a classic veal entree, piquant with lemon.*

Menu for 6

- **Prosciutto-Wrapped Breadsticks**
- **Veal Piccata**
  Fresh Asparagus Tips
  Hard Rolls
- **Tomato Wedges and Marinated Artichoke Hearts on Red Lettuce**
- **Quick Cherries Jubilee**

SHOPPING LIST

- ☐ ¼ pound prosciutto, thinly sliced
- ☐ 2 pounds veal scallops
- ☐ 1 bunch fresh parsley
- ☐ 1 head red lettuce
- ☐ 2 pounds fresh asparagus
- ☐ 3 or 4 tomatoes
- ☐ 1 lemon
- ☐ 1 small jar marinated artichoke hearts
- ☐ 1 16-ounce can pitted dark sweet cherries
- ☐ 12 breadsticks
- ☐ 1 quart vanilla ice cream

Have on Hand
- ☐ All-purpose flour

- ☐ Salt
- ☐ Pepper
- ☐ Salad oil
- ☐ Lemon juice
- ☐ Butter or margarine
- ☐ Brandy or kirsch

SCHEDULE

1. Prepare Prosciutto-Wrapped Breadsticks.
2. Assemble salad.
3. Cook asparagus.
4. Prepare Veal Piccata.
5. Prepare Quick Cherries Jubilee.

Prosciutto-Wrapped Breadsticks

6   thin slices prosciutto
12   bread sticks

Cut prosciutto slices in half crosswise. Place a bread stick at the cut side of each slice. Roll up and stack in serving basket, seam side down.

Veal Piccata

2   *pounds veal scallops, pounded very thin*
4   *tablespoons salad oil*
1/2   *cup all-purpose flour*
1/2   *teaspoon salt*
    Dash pepper
3   *tablespoons lemon juice*
3   *tablespoons water*
1/2   *cup butter*
2   *tablespoons chopped parsley*
1   *lemon, thinly sliced*

Cut veal into six serving-sized pieces. In large heavy skillet heat oil over medium-high heat. In shallow dish or pan mix flour with salt and pepper. Dredge veal in flour mixture and saute 2 minutes on each side, until cooked through but not brown. Transfer to heated serving platter. Pour excess oil from skillet. Add lemon juice and water; stir well, scraping brown bits from skillet. Add butter and melt over medium-high heat, stirring 2 minutes. Add parsley. Pour sauce over veal. Garnish each serving with lemon slice.

Quick Cherries Jubilee

1   *quart vanilla ice cream*
1   *can (16 1/2 oz.) pitted dark sweet cherries*
6   *tablespoons brandy or kirsch*

Place 2 scoops vanilla ice cream in each serving dish. In small saucepan combine cherries and brandy or kirsch; heat. Ignite with long-handled match; immediately pour over ice cream.

SCALLOPINI VARIATION

The lemon juice gives this veal dish the name Piccata. For another version, substitute 1/2 cup vermouth for the lemon juice and boil 2 minutes, scraping up browned bits. Reduce by nearly half, add 1 tablespoon capers and 2 tablespoons minced parsley. Serve over veal.

Beef Stroganoff, page 54

Sweet and Sour Beef, page 56   *Chicken Amandine, page 58* ▶

Beef Stroganoff
TENDER CUBE STEAK IN SOUR CREAM SAUCE

This family-style dinner for guests centers on a hearty Russian favorite.

Menu for 6

- **Beef Stroganoff**
  Egg Noodles
  Cucumber-Onion-
  Tomato Salad

French Bread
with Butter
- **Black Forest**
  Sundaes

SHOPPING LIST

- 1½ pounds beef cube steaks
- 1 head lettuce
- 1 medium cucumber
- 1 white or yellow onion
- 1 red onion
- 3 tomatoes
- ⅓ pound mushrooms
- 1 bunch fresh basil or dried basil
- 1 bunch fresh dill or dillweed
- ☐ Fresh or canned cherries
- 1 13¾- or 14½-ounce can beef broth
- 1 16-ounce package egg noodles
- 1 package chocolate cookies
- 1 loaf French bread
- 1 8-ounce container sour cream
- ½ pint heavy or whipping cream
- 1 quart cherry vanilla ice cream

Have on Hand
- Sugar
- Cornstarch
- Salt
- Pepper
- Garlic
- White vinegar
- Butter or margarine
- Chocolate syrup
- White wine
- Kirsch

SCHEDULE

1. Prepare and marinate cucumbers and onions for salad.
2. Prepare topping for Black Forest Sundaes; chill.
3. Cook egg noodles.
4. Prepare Beef Stroganoff.
5. Assemble salad.

Beef Stroganoff

4½ tablespoons butter or
    margarine
1½ pounds beef cube steaks,
    cut into strips
1½ garlic cloves, crushed
⅓ pound mushrooms, sliced
1 small onion, minced
¾ cup beef broth
⅓ cup white wine
1 tablespoon chopped fresh
    dill or ½ teaspoon
    dillweed
¼ teaspoon salt
⅛ teaspoon pepper
1 tablespoon cornstarch
¾ cup sour cream

In large skillet melt butter or margarine.
Add beef and sear on all sides; remove
and set aside. In drippings saute garlic
and mushrooms about 3 minutes. Return
meat to skillet and stir in onion.

In small bowl combine broth, wine, dill
or dillweed, salt, pepper and cornstarch.
Stir into skillet. Boil 1 minute. Remove
from heat and stir in sour cream. Spoon
over cooked egg noodles.

Black Forest Sundaes

¾ cup chocolate syrup
3 tablespoons kirsch
1 quart cherry vanilla ice
    cream
½ cup heavy or whipping
    cream, whipped and
    sweetened to taste
6 chocolate cookies,
    crumbled
    Fresh or canned cherries,
    for garnish

In small bowl mix chocolate syrup with
brandy or kirsch. Place 1 or 2 scoops ice
cream in each serving dish. Top each
serving with brandy-syrup mixture, a dollop of whipped cream and a sprinkle of
chocolate cookie crumbs. Garnish with a
cherry.

MUSHROOM TIPS

*Choose mushrooms that are firm and
smooth, with no space between the
stem and cap.*

- *Size has nothing to do with quality;
choose the size most suitable for
your recipe.*
- *Refrigerate mushrooms, loosely
wrapped, in paper bag or card-
board container; cover with damp
towel to keep fresh. Airtight storage
will cause mushrooms to rot.*
- *Age darkens mushrooms, but a
sprinkling of lemon juice will help
keep them white.*

Sweet and Sour Beef

CELEBRATE WITH A CHANUKAH DINNER

Traditional Chanukah foods—like Sweet and Sour Beef and Potato Latkes—are the center of this winter holiday meal. Delicious as a complement to meat or fish, these onion-flavored potato pancakes also make a satisfying lunch. Or serve them with plenty of applesauce for a hearty breakfast.

Menu for 6

- **Sweet and Sour Beef**
- **Potato Latkes**
- **Holiday Red Cabbage**
- **Steamed Carrots**
- **Honey Cake**

SHOPPING LIST

- ☐ 2 pounds beef cube steaks
- ☐ 1½ pounds potatoes
- ☐ 1 medium onion
- ☐ 1 pound carrots
- ☐ 1 13¾- or 14½-ounce can beef broth
- ☐ 2 16-ounce jars red cabbage
- ☐ 1 8-ounce jar applesauce
- ☐ 1 small box ginger snaps
- ☐ 1 honey cake

Have on Hand

- ☐ All-purpose flour
- ☐ Baking powder
- ☐ Dark brown sugar
- ☐ Salt
- ☐ Pepper

- ☐ Whole cloves
- ☐ Bay leaves
- ☐ Cinnamon
- ☐ Allspice
- ☐ Garlic
- ☐ Salad oil
- ☐ Cider vinegar
- ☐ Eggs

SCHEDULE

1. Prepare Sweet and Sour Beef.
2. Cook carrots.
3. Combine ingredients for Holiday Red Cabbage; heat through.
4. Prepare Potato Latkes.

Sweet and Sour Beef

3/4 cup all-purpose flour
1/2 teaspoon salt
     Dash pepper
2   pounds beef cube steaks
3   tablespoons salad oil
1   can (13³/4 or 14¹/2 oz.) beef
     broth
2/3 cup cider vinegar
1   garlic clove, pressed
3   whole cloves
1   bay leaf
1/3 cup dark brown sugar
5   ginger snaps
3   to 4 teaspoons water

In pie plate combine flour, salt and pepper. Dredge beef in flour; shake off excess. In large skillet heat oil over medium-high heat. Brown steaks on both sides. Add beef broth, vinegar, garlic, cloves, bay leaf and brown sugar. Bring to a boil and cook over high heat 5 minutes. Reduce heat, cover and cook 20 minutes. Transfer steaks to serving platter. Add crumbled ginger snaps and water to sauce in skillet. Whisk to dissolve. Taste for seasoning. Pour sauce over steaks to serve.

Potato Latkes

1¹/2 pounds unpeeled potatoes
1   medium onion
1/3 cup boiling water
1   egg, beaten
1/4 cup all-purpose flour

1/2 teaspoon salt
1/4 teaspoon baking powder
1/8 teaspoon pepper
     Salad oil

In food processor shred potatoes and onion. Replace shredder with steel knife; process 20 seconds. Drain off liquid. In bowl combine shredded potatoes and onion with boiling water; stir. Add egg, flour, salt, baking powder and pepper; stir well. Heat enough salad oil to cover bottom of large skillet. Drop batter in by tablespoonfuls. Cook until golden brown on both sides; drain on paper towels.

Holiday Red Cabbage

2   jars (16 oz. each) red
     cabbage
1/2 cup applesauce
1/8 teaspoon cinnamon
1/8 teaspoon allspice

In medium saucepan combine red cabbage, applesauce, cinnamon and allspice and heat through.

VINEGAR TIPS

Vinegar plus brown sugar equals sweet-and-sour; vinegar plus oil equals salad dressing, but vinegar has many other uses as well.

• A few drops in cooking water keeps cabbage odor from drifting.

• Sprinkle on fried potatoes or fried fish.

Chicken Breasts Amandine

DINNER WITH A SWEETHEART OF A DESSERT

Here is a perfect meal to serve on Valentine's Day or an anniversary. Although the dishes look and taste like party fare, they are simple and speedy.

Menu for 6

- **Chicken Breasts Amandine**
- **Fuss-Free Risotto**

Buttered Green Beans
- **Quick Cherry Crisp**

SHOPPING LIST

- ☐ 6 chicken cutlets
- ☐ 1½ pounds fresh green beans
- ☐ 1 21-ounce can cherry pie filling
- ☐ 1 small can or package sliced almonds
- ☐ 1 16-ounce container half and half cream
- ☐ 1 8-ounce container frozen whipped topping made with real cream

Have on Hand
- ☐ All-purpose flour
- ☐ Long-grain rice
- ☐ Brown sugar
- ☐ Salt
- ☐ Pepper
- ☐ Cinnamon
- ☐ Rosemary
- ☐ Salad oil
- ☐ Parmesan cheese
- ☐ Butter or margarine

SCHEDULE

1. Prepare Quick Cherry Crisp.
2. Cook rice.
3. Cook green beans.
4. Prepare Chicken Breasts Amandine.
5. Prepare Fuss-Free Risotto.

Chicken Breasts Amandine

3   tablespoons butter or
        margarine, divided
¾   cup sliced almonds
½   teaspoon salt
1   teaspoon rosemary
¼   teaspoon pepper
⅓   cup all-purpose flour
6   chicken cutlets
1½   tablespoons salad oil

In large skillet melt 1½ tablespoons butter or margarine. Add almonds and cook until golden; remove and set aside. In flat dish combine salt, rosemary, pepper and flour. Coat chicken breasts in flour mixture. In same skillet heat remaining butter with salad oil. Cook chicken about 7 minutes on each side. Sprinkle with toasted almonds.

Fuss-Free Risotto

2¼   cups water
1   cup long-grain rice
3   tablespoons butter or
        margarine
½   cup half and half cream
¾   cup grated Parmesan
        cheese
     Dash salt

In saucepan bring water to a boil. Stir in rice. Reduce heat; cover and simmer 15 to 20 minutes. Stir in butter or margarine, half and half, Parmesan and salt.

Quick Cherry Crisp

1   can (21 oz.) cherry pie
        filling
¾   cup all-purpose flour
3   tablespoons brown sugar
¼   teaspoon cinnamon
6   tablespoons butter or
        margarine
     Frozen whipped topping
        made with real cream,
        thawed

Preheat oven to 450° F. Spoon cherry pie filling into a pie plate. In medium bowl combine flour, brown sugar and cinnamon. With pastry blender, cut butter or margarine into flour until mixture resembles peas. Sprinkle over filling. Bake 15 minutes. Reduce heat to 375° F.; bake 10 minutes. Serve with whipped topping.

BUYING RICE

Four main types of rice are widely available.
- Regular rice *is cleaned and graded as short-, medium- or long-grain.*
- Parboiled rice *is steamed before milling, making the grains fluffier when cooked.*
- Precooked rice *requires less moisture and time for cooking.*
- Brown rice *retains most of its outer bran layer for chewier texture and nuttier taste.*
- Wild rice *isn't really rice at all, but the seed of a wild grass.*

Skewered Shrimp, page 62

Skewered Shrimp

LIGHT, JUST RIGHT COMPANY DINNER

Your guests will love this skewered shrimp entree because it's delicious—and you will love it because it's quick and easy. Paired with cherry tomatoes and marinated in a lemon sauce, this dish goes well with our Piquant Rice and Stir-Fried Snow Peas.

Menu for 6

- **Skewered Shrimp**
- **Piquant Rice**
- **Stir-Fried Snow Peas**

Lemon Sherbet with Kiwi Slices

SHOPPING LIST

- ☐ 1½ pounds medium shrimp, shelled and deveined
- ☐ ¾ pound fresh snow peas or 2 6-ounce packages frozen snow peas
- ☐ 1 or 2 pints cherry tomatoes (18 cherry tomatoes)
- ☐ 1 onion
- ☐ 2 lemons
- ☐ 2 kiwi fruit
- ☐ 1 bunch fresh dill or dillweed
- ☐ 2 8-ounce bottles clam juice
- ☐ 1 quart lemon sherbet

Have on Hand
- ☐ Long-grain rice

- ☐ Sugar
- ☐ Salt
- ☐ Garlic
- ☐ Butter or margarine
- ☐ Red pepper sauce
- ☐ Salad oil

SCHEDULE

1. Assemble and marinate Shrimp on Skewers.
2. Start cooking Piquant Rice.
3. Broil Shrimp on Skewers.
4. Prepare Stir-Fried Snow Peas.

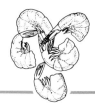

Skewered Shrimp

3	tablespoons salad oil
1/3	cup lemon juice
2	garlic cloves, pressed
1	tablespoon chopped fresh dill or 1 teaspoon dried dillweed
4	dashes red pepper sauce
1/8	teaspoon salt
1 1/2	pounds medium shrimp, shelled and deveined
18	cherry tomatoes, stems removed

Line jelly-roll pan with foil. In small bowl stir together salad oil, lemon juice, garlic, dill, red pepper sauce and salt. Thread shrimp and tomatoes alternately on six metal skewers. Place on jelly-roll pan. Pour lemon-dill sauce over skewers and marinate 15 minutes, turning twice. Broil in jelly-roll pan 4 minutes on each side, basting frequently. Serve remaining sauce over rice.

Piquant Rice

3	tablespoons butter or margarine
3	tablespoons chopped onion
1 1/2	cups long-grain rice
1 1/2	cups clam juice
1 1/2	cups water
1 1/2	teaspoons slivered lemon peel

In large skillet melt butter or margarine. Add chopped onion and saute until trans-lucent, about 3 minutes. Add rice; saute just until golden. Gradually add clam juice and water, stirring once. Reduce heat, cover and simmer until rice is tender and water has been absorbed, 15 to 20 minutes. Toss with slivered lemon peel.

Stir-Fried Snow Peas

3/4	pound fresh snow peas, washed and trimmed or 2 packages (6 oz. each) frozen pea pods, unthawed
3	tablespoons salad oil
1/2	teaspoon salt
1/2	teaspoon sugar
3	tablespoons water

In large skillet heat salad oil over me-dium-high heat. Add snow peas and stir-fry until coated, about 30 seconds. Add salt, sugar and water; stir. Cover and cook 1 to 2 minutes until snow peas are tender-crisp.

HOT CHERRY TOMATO APPETIZER

Trim cherry tomatoes and squeeze out seeds and pulp. Brush large mushroom caps with melted butter and broil 3 minutes; fill each center with sour cream and a plump to-mato; broil 1 minute more.

Clusters of Candles

Candle arrangements always say "party." Holders needn't match: You can use glass, brass, silver, wood or ceramic of different sizes and shapes. Use candles of one color, or mix colors at random. But remember:

- *Don't burn candles near fresh or dried flowers, pinecones, fir sprays or other flammables without hurricane-type glass covers. Even then, be sure that the flammables don't touch the glass.*
- *Arrange candles in more than one area only if you can be sure to keep an eye on them. Don't count on guests to watch for drips.*
- *Locate candles out of the way of drafts from windows, doors, air conditioning and warm-air heating systems. On a buffet table, candles should be placed where people won't have to reach around or over them and risk burning their sleeves.*
- *Extinguish drippy candles. If liquid wax falls on a tablecloth, bare wood or rug, save cleanup for after the party when wax dries. (To remove wax, apply ice to "stiffen," then lift with a dull knife. If a stain remains, cover with blotting paper and press with a warm iron.)*

Easy and Pleasing Tricks with Frozen Peas

A 10-oz. package of frozen peas serves as the basis for the following dishes.

- Nippy Dip: *Fill blender container with thawed peas, a 3-oz. package of cream cheese, ½ cup sour cream, 2 tablespoons chopped onion, 1 tablespoon chopped green chilies; blend smooth. Chill.*

- St. Patrick Soup: *Puree in blender two packages thawed peas, ½ cup sour cream, ½ cup chicken broth. Chill.*
- Peppy Peas: *Season with chopped fresh or dried mint, lemon-pepper or poppy seeds.*

Special Tips for Special Events

- *Centerpieces of flowers, fruit and candles shouldn't obstruct the view across the table, or be overpowering in aroma. Consider silk flowers—a good investment.*
- *Start the evening off with the dishwasher empty so that dishes can disappear between courses. Clear out trash container, dish drainers, sink, too.*
- *If you offer jug wines, serve from handsome decanters or pitchers.*
- *Feed children, baby-sitter, before guests arrive.*

Party Foods/Headache Foods

Do parties give you headaches? The following foods contain the substance tyramine, which causes headaches for some people. But while tyramine can have deleterious effects, it's also a natural stimulant and a great talk inducer, giving the items below a reputation as super party foods.
- *Aged cheese*
- *Pickled herring*
- *Chicken livers*
- *Sour cream*
- *Beer*
- *Champagne*
- *Aged beef*
- *Chocolate*
- *Ripe bananas*
- *Soy sauce*
- *Sherry or red wine, especially Chianti*

Quick and Easy Orange-Flavored Vegetables

For zesty flavor and color, stir frozen orange juice concentrate a tablespoon at a time into carrots, parsnips, zucchini or summer squash.

Pork Chops with Lime Sauce

PERENNIAL FAVORITES AT THEIR BEST

You'll love the fresh lime sauce that makes this pork chop dish so special. Try it over chicken and turkey cutlets as well.

Menu for 6

- **Pork Chops with Lime Sauce**
- **Cranberry Fruit Relish**
- **Fine Egg Noodles**
- **Peppery Brussels Sprouts**
- **Walnut Cake**

SHOPPING LIST

- ☐ 6 pork chops, ³/₄ inch thick
- ☐ 1 13³/₄- or 14¹/₂-ounce can chicken broth
- ☐ 1 large or 2 small limes
- ☐ 1 lemon
- ☐ 2 10-ounce containers fresh Brussel sprouts
- ☐ 1 12-ounce package fresh cranberries
- ☐ 1 apple
- ☐ 1 8-ounce can crushed pineapple in juice
- ☐ 1 medium orange
- ☐ Prepared or frozen walnut cake

Have on Hand
- ☐ Salt
- ☐ Pepper

- ☐ Cracked pepper or black peppercorns
- ☐ Salad oil
- ☐ Brown sugar
- ☐ Dijon mustard
- ☐ Cornstarch
- ☐ Butter or margarine
- ☐ Raisins
- ☐ Orange juice
- ☐ Sugar
- ☐ Fine egg noodles

SCHEDULE

1. Prepare Cranberry Fruit Relish.
2. Prepare Pork Chops with Lime Sauce.
3. Cook noodles.
4. Prepare Peppery Brussels Sprouts.

Pork Chops with Lime Sauce

6   pork chops, ³/₄ inch thick
¹/₄   teaspoon salt
      Dash pepper
1¹/₂   tablespoons salad oil
1   cup chicken broth
1¹/₂   tablespoons brown sugar
1¹/₂   teaspoons Dijon mustard
4   tablespoons fresh lime
      juice, divided
1   tablespoon cornstarch
¹/₃   cup water
2   tablespoons butter or margarine

Sprinkle chops with salt and pepper. In large skillet heat oil. Add chops and brown on both sides. Add broth, brown sugar, mustard and half of the lime juice. Cover and simmer 20 minutes. Transfer chops to serving platter. In small bowl stir cornstarch into water; add to skillet. Bring to a boil; boil 1 minute. Remove from heat. Swirl in remaining lime juice and butter or margarine. Pour over chops.

Cranberry Fruit Relish

2   cups fresh cranberries
1   apple, peeled and chopped
¹/₃   cup raisins
¹/₄   cup orange juice
1   tablespoon sugar
1   can (8 oz.) crushed pine-
      apple in juice, undrained
1   medium orange, peeled
      and cut into sections

In medium saucepan combine cranberries, apple, raisins, orange juice and sugar. Bring to a boil. Cover and simmer 20 minutes or until cranberries pop. Remove from heat. Stir in crushed pineapple and orange sections. Serve warm or chill in freezer.

Peppery Brussels Sprouts

2   tablespoons butter or
      margarine
¹/₂   teaspoon cracked black pepper
2   containers (10 oz. each)
      fresh Brussels sprouts,
      trimmed
¹/₄   teaspoon salt
¹/₂   cup water
2   teaspoons fresh lemon juice

In medium skillet melt butter or margarine over medium heat. Add pepper and saute 1 minute. Add sprouts and toss well. Sprinkle on salt and water; cover and cook over medium-low heat about 8 minutes. Uncover, sprinkle with lemon juice and toss.

THE FRESHEST BRUSSELS SPROUTS

• *When you see fresh Brussels sprouts on the stalk at the farmers' market or your local greengrocer, buy some and serve them the same day.*

• *Break or trim off each sprout from the stalk, starting at the base.*

Chicken Yakitori

JAPANESE-STYLE BARBECUE

Whether cooked on a backyard grill or under the broiler, this meal will please everyone.

Menu for 6

- **Shrimp-Bacon Appetizers**
- **Chicken Yakitori**
- **Rice**
- **Tossed Salad with Garlic-Oregano Dressing**

Fresh Pineapple Chunks

SHOPPING LIST

- ☐ 6   chicken cutlets
- ☐ 1   pound medium shrimp (about 25 shrimp)
- ☐ 1   pound bacon
- ☐ 1   bunch green onions
- ☐ 2   red peppers
- ☐ 1   large head romaine lettuce
- ☐ 1   large cucumber
- ☐ 1   pint cherry tomatoes
- ☐ 1   large pineapple
- ☐ 1   lemon or lemon juice
- ☐ 1   bottle sesame oil
- ☐ 1   2 1/2-ounce jar sesame seed

Have on Hand

- ☐   Long-grain rice
- ☐   Sugar
- ☐   Salt
- ☐   Pepper

- ☐   Oregano
- ☐   Garlic
- ☐   Wine vinegar
- ☐   Salad oil
- ☐   Soy sauce

SCHEDULE

1. Cut pineapple into serving-size pieces (see Tips); cover and refrigerate.
2. Cook rice.
3. Prepare skewers and sauce for Chicken Yakitori.
4. Mix salad dressing; prepare vegetables.
5. Prepare and serve Shrimp-Bacon Appetizers.
6. Cook Chicken Yakitori.

Shrimp-Bacon Appetizers

1   *pound sliced bacon*
1   *pound medium shrimp*
     (about 25), shelled and
     deveined

Preheat broiler. Cut each bacon strip in half crosswise. Wrap each shrimp in a piece of bacon. Broil 10 minutes, turning once. Serve on picks.

Chicken Yakitori

½   *cup sesame oil*
½   *cup sesame seed*
1½ *tablespoons lemon juice*
1   *tablespoon soy sauce*
6   *chicken cutlets*
1   *bunch green onions, cut*
     into 2-inch pieces
2   *red peppers, cut in 2-inch*
     chunks

Preheat broiler. Place sesame oil, sesame seed, lemon juice and soy sauce in blender. Puree until smooth. Allow to stand at room temperature a few minutes.

Cut each chicken cutlet into 4 pieces. Arrange chicken, green onions and red peppers alternately on 6 metal skewers. Brush with sesame sauce. Grill or broil about 4 minutes on each side, basting several times with sauce.

Tossed Salad with Garlic-Oregano Dressing

½   *cup salad oil*
3   *tablespoons wine*
     vinegar
1   *garlic clove, crushed*
½   *teaspoon oregano*
½   *teaspoon salt*
⅛   *teaspoon pepper*
     Pinch sugar
1   *large head romaine lettuce,*
     torn
1   *large cucumber, peeled*
     and sliced
1   *pint cherry tomatoes*

In jar with tight-fitting lid, shake oil and vinegar with garlic, oregano, salt, pepper and sugar. Pour dressing over vegetables and toss well.

PINEAPPLE TIPS

• *How can you tell when a pineapple is ripe enough to eat? Tug on one of the middle leaves. If it pulls out easily, the pineapple is ripe.*

• *To serve pineapple chunks in the shell, slice the fruit in half lengthwise, leaves and all, with a long, sharp knife. Scoop out fruit with grapefruit knife. Remove hard core and eyes with paring knife. Return cut fruit to shell for serving.*

Sesame Baked Fish

A LIGHT AND SIMPLE SEAFOOD MENU

This scrumptious sesame-seed-topped fish entree bakes in the oven while you prepare the vegetable and a show-stopping dessert. If you sometimes have trouble finding fresh fish, by all means use frozen; our Tips should help you out.

Menu for 6

- **Sesame Baked Fish**
  Small Red Potatoes
- **Orange-Flavored Peas**
- **Viennese Torte**

SHOPPING LIST

- ☐ 2 pounds fresh cod or other white fish fillets
- ☐ 1½ pounds new potatoes
- ☐ 1 bunch fresh parsley
- ☐ 1 large lemon
- ☐ 1 small can or package slivered almonds
- ☐ 1 2½-ounce jar sesame seed
- ☐ 1 pound cake
- ☐ 1 8-ounce container sour cream
- ☐ 2 10-ounce packages frozen peas

Have on Hand
- ☐ Bread (for bread crumbs)

- ☐ Confectioners' sugar
- ☐ Salt
- ☐ Pepper
- ☐ Eggs
- ☐ Butter or margarine
- ☐ Orange marmalade
- ☐ Seedless raspberry jam
- ☐ Vanilla extract

SCHEDULE

1. Prepare Sesame Baked Fish.
2. Cook potatoes.
3. Prepare Orange-Flavored Peas.
4. Prepare Viennese Torte.

Sesame Baked Fish

½   cup sesame seed
1½ cups fresh bread crumbs
2   pounds cod or other white
      fish fillets
1   large lemon
¼   teaspoon salt
     Dash pepper
2   eggs
2   tablespoons water
4   teaspoons butter or
      margarine

Preheat oven to 350° F. In jelly-roll pan combine sesame seed and bread crumbs. Toast in oven 8 minutes, stirring once, until golden brown. Butter an 8-inch baking dish; set aside. Cut fillets diagonally into 6 pieces. Squeeze lemon juice on both sides; sprinkle with salt and pepper.

In shallow bowl beat eggs with water. Dip fish in egg, then coat with sesame-crumb mixture. Arrange in baking dish. Sprinkle remaining crumb mixture on fish. Top each piece with a dab of butter or margarine. Bake fresh fish about 15 to 20 minutes, frozen approximately 25 to 30 minutes or until fish flakes easily when tested with a fork.

Orange-Flavored Peas

2   packages (10 oz. each)
      frozen peas

4   tablespoons orange
      marmalade
2   tablespoons butter or
      margarine
     Salt
     Pepper

Cook peas according to package directions; drain. Return to saucepan; stir in marmalade, butter or margarine and salt and pepper to taste. Heat until butter melts.

Viennese Torte

½   cup sour cream
1   tablespoon confectioners'
      sugar
½   teaspoon vanilla extract
1   pound cake
½   cup seedless raspberry jam

In small bowl combine sour cream, confectioners' sugar and vanilla extract. Cut pound cake into 4 horizontal layers. Spread each layer with raspberry jam; stack layers. Spread sour cream mixture lavishly on top.

SAUTEED FROZEN FISH FILLETS

The secret of successfully serving frozen fish fillets is to not thaw them completely. Remove fish from package and place at room temperature 15 minutes to partially thaw. Using a serrated knife, slice fillets crosswise on the diagonal. Dip in egg, then flour. Heat oil in skillet and cook fish 3 to 5 minutes on each side.

Chicken Livers in Sour Cream

AN ENTREE IN THE GRAND RUSSIAN STYLE

This rich stroganoff meal features chicken livers instead of the usual beef.

═══ Menu for 6 ═══

- **Chicken Livers in Sour Cream Buttered Noodles**

- **Sauteed Carrots with Walnuts Spinach Salad**
- **Viennese Sundaes**

SHOPPING LIST

- ☐ 1½ pounds chicken livers
- ☐ 2 10-ounce packages fresh spinach
- ☐ 1½ pounds carrots
- ☐ 1 red onion
- ☐ 2 medium onions
- ☐ 1 bunch fresh parsley
- ☐ 2 16-ounce cans apricot halves
- ☐ 1 small can or package chopped walnuts
- ☐ 1 small can or package chopped hazelnuts or filberts
- ☐ 1 16-ounce package egg noodles
- ☐ 1 16-ounce container sour cream
- ☐ 1 quart lemon sherbet
- ☐ Apricot brandy

Have on Hand

- ☐ Bacon
- ☐ Sugar
- ☐ Salt
- ☐ Pepper
- ☐ Bottled salad dressing
- ☐ Butter or margarine
- ☐ Chicken bouillon cubes

SCHEDULE

1. Marinate apricot halves for Viennese Sundaes.
2. Prepare Sauteed Carrots with Walnuts.
3. Cook egg noodles.
4. Prepare spinach salad.
5. Prepare Chicken Livers in Sour Cream.

Chicken Livers in Sour Cream

1½ cups sliced onions
1½ tablespoons butter or
       margarine
1½ pounds chicken livers
       Dash pepper
1   chicken bouillon cube
½   cup water
1½ cups sour cream
       Fresh parsley

In large skillet saute onions in butter or margarine until translucent. Add chicken livers and pepper. Saute 8 to 10 minutes. Dissolve bouillon cube in water; add to skillet. Stir in sour cream and heat through. Serve over noodles.

Viennese Sundaes

¾   cup apricot brandy
⅓   cup sugar
2   cans (16 oz. each) apricot
       halves, drained
1   quart lemon sherbet
¾   cup chopped hazelnuts or
       walnuts

In large bowl mix brandy, sugar and apricot halves. Marinate 20 minutes.

Place 1 scoop lemon sherbet in each dessert dish. Add 1 or 2 apricot halves and some of the brandy, then another scoop of sherbet. Top with more apricots and brandy and sprinkle with chopped nuts.

Sauteed Carrots with Walnuts

1½ pounds carrots, peeled
       and sliced
½   teaspoon salt
3   tablespoons butter or
       margarine
½   cup chopped walnuts
1   teaspoon sugar

In medium saucepan cook carrots in salted water to cover. Drain and set aside. In same saucepan melt butter or margarine. Add walnuts and sugar. Saute 1 minute. Add carrots and toss to coat. Heat through.

ADD VARIETY TO FRESH SPINACH SALAD

Toss in some:
- *crisp, crumbled bacon*
- *sliced hard-cooked eggs*
- *crunchy bean sprouts*
- *very thinly sliced red or white onion rings*
- *marinated mushrooms*
- *garlic-flavored croutons*
- *crumbled blue cheese*
- *mandarin oranges*

Sauteed Flounder Rolls with Noodles

DELICIOUS FRESH FISH DINNER

Here is a menu that makes the most of fresh, delicious foods for dishes that look as good as they taste.

Menu for 6

- **Sauteed Flounder Rolls with Noodles**
- **Fresh Fruit with Devonshire Cream**

Green Peas and Baby Onions

SHOPPING LIST

- ☐ 6   flounder fillets about 1½ pounds
- ☐ 3   medium tomatoes
- ☐ 1   onion
- ☐ 1   bunch parsley
- ☐   Selection of fresh fruit
- ☐ 1   16-ounce package medium egg noodles
- ☐ 1   8-ounce package cream cheese
- ☐ ½   pint heavy or whipping cream
- ☐ 2   10-ounce packages frozen peas and baby onions

Have on Hand

- ☐   Sugar
- ☐   Confectioners' sugar

- ☐   Salt
- ☐   Pepper
- ☐   Garlic
- ☐ 1   lemon or lemon juice
- ☐   White vinegar
- ☐   Butter or margarine
- ☐   All-purpose flour
- ☐   Vanilla extract
- ☐   Dry white wine

SCHEDULE

1. Cook Sauteed Flounder with Noodles.
2. Cook frozen peas and baby onions.
3. Prepare Fruit with Devonshire Cream.

Sauteed Flounder Rolls with Noodles

6 flounder fillets (about
    1½ pounds)
¼ teaspoon salt
    Dash pepper
2 tablespoons lemon juice
3 tablespoons butter or
    margarine
⅓ cup chopped onion
1 cup dry white wine
3 cups peeled, coarsely
    chopped tomatoes (about
    3 medium tomatoes)
3 tablespoons finely chopped
    parsley
    Pinch sugar
3 cups medium egg noodles
1 tablespoon all-purpose flour
1 tablespoon water

Sprinkle fish fillets lightly with salt, pepper and lemon juice; roll up. In large skillet heat butter or margarine; add onion and saute until translucent. Add fish, wine, tomatoes, parsley and sugar. Bring to a boil, cover and simmer gently 8 to 10 minutes or until fish flakes easily when tested with a fork.

Meanwhile, cook noodles according to package directions; drain and transfer to heated platter. With slotted spoon transfer fish fillets to noodles; keep warm. In small bowl combine flour and water to make a smooth paste. Stir into liquid in skillet. Cook over medium heat, whisking constantly until thickened. Pour over fish and noodles.

Fresh Fruit with Devonshire Cream

1 package (8 oz.) cream
    cheese, softened
1 cup heavy or whipping
    cream
¼ teaspoon vanilla extract
    Confectioners' sugar
    Selection of fresh fruit (see
    below)

In medium bowl beat cheese until creamy. Gradually beat in cream. Add vanilla and confectioners' sugar to taste. Serve with strawberries, pineapple chunks, apple slices, orange sections, grapes, sliced bananas or other fresh fruit.

START WITH A PACKAGE OF CREAM CHEESE . . .

- *Serve cream cheese and guava shells on plain crackers.*
- *Stir into hot mashed potatoes until melted; add snipped chives.*
- *Spread on slices of French bread, broil until lightly browned; sprinkle with sliced tomatoes and chopped green onions.*

Mexicali Chicken

A COLORFUL AND TASTY CHICKEN DINNER

For a hearty and colorful change of pace, add this avocado and cheese surprise to your repertoire of chicken recipes.

Menu for 4

- **Mexicali Chicken Rice with Chopped Parsley and Cilantro**

Tossed Green Salad with
- **Fast Vinaigrette**
- **Pistachio Macaroon Pudding**

SHOPPING LIST

- ☐ 4 chicken cutlets
- ☐ 1 small avocado
- ☐ Salad greens
- ☐ 1 bunch fresh parsley
- ☐ 1 bunch fresh cilantro
- ☐ 1 regular-size package pistachio instant pudding
- ☐ 1 4-ounce can green chilies
- ☐ 1 small package soft macaroons
- ☐ 8 ounces Monterey Jack cheese
- ☐ 1 8-ounce container sour cream

Have on Hand
- ☐ Long-grain rice
- ☐ Sugar
- ☐ Salt
- ☐ Pepper

- ☐ Milk
- ☐ Butter or margarine
- ☐ Salad oil
- ☐ Vinegar
- ☐ Dijon mustard

SCHEDULE

1. Cook rice; combine with parsley and cilantro.
2. Mix Fast Vinaigrette; prepare salad greens.
3. Prepare Pistachio Macaroon Pudding; refrigerate.
4. Cook Mexicali Chicken.

Mexicali Chicken

4 chicken cutlets
2 tablespoons butter or
   margarine
1/3 cup sour cream
1 canned green chili,
   drained and finely
   chopped
1/2 cup shredded Monterey
   Jack cheese
1 small avocado, peeled and
   sliced

Place chicken cutlets between two sheets of wax paper; pound to 1/4- to 1/2-inch thickness.

In medium skillet heat butter or margarine over medium-high heat. Saute chicken cutlets about 3 minutes on each side. Remove chicken and place on foil-lined broiler tray.

In small bowl mix sour cream, green chili and cheese until well blended; spread 1 rounded tablespoon on each chicken piece. Broil 5 minutes in preheated broiler with rack about 6 inches from heat. Garnish with avocado slices.

Fast Vinaigrette

3 tablespoons salad oil
1 tablespoon vinegar
1 teaspoon Dijon mustard
1/4 teaspoon salt
1/4 teaspoon sugar
   Dash pepper

Combine all ingredients in jar with tight-fitting lid; cover and shake vigorously.

Pistachio Macaroon Pudding

1 package (regular size)
   pistachio instant
   pudding
1/2 cup crumbled soft
   macaroons

Prepare pudding according to package directions. Stir in macaroons and pour into 4 individual dishes. Refrigerate until ready to serve.

AVOCADO TIPS

• *To test an avocado for ripeness, press one finger gently against the roundest part of the fruit. If this pressure leaves a slight indentation, the avocado is ripe.*

• *To halve an avocado, cut it lengthwise, working knife around pit, and twist apart. Cradle one half in hand and carefully press knife into pit, twisting to remove cleanly.*

• *To prevent avocado from becoming discolored after peeling, sprinkle with lemon juice.*

Currant-Glazed Lamb Chops

PARTY LAMB CHOPS WITH A RUBY GLAZE

A smooth blender soup is a perfect overture to the glazed lamb chops that follow.

Menu for 6

- **Chilled Cucumber-Watercress Soup**
- **Currant-Glazed Lamb Chops New Potatoes**

- **Green Salad with Romano Dressing**
  Vanilla Ice Cream with Amaretto and Macaroons

SHOPPING LIST

☐ 6 to 12	loin lamp chops, 1½ inches thick	
☐ 1	bunch watercress	
☐ 2	medium cucumbers	
☐ 1	onion	
☐ 1½	pounds new potatoes	
☐ 2	heads Bibb lettuce	
☐ 1	green pepper	
☐ 1	medium red onion	
☐ 1	package macaroons	
☐ 1	3-ounce jar grated Romano cheese	
☐ 1	16-ounce container sour cream	
☐ 1	quart vanilla ice cream	

Have on Hand

☐   Salt

☐   Pepper
☐   Garlic
☐ 1   lemon or lemon juice
☐   Salad oil
☐   Cider vinegar
☐   Milk
☐   Red currant jelly
☐   Amaretto

SCHEDULE

1. Prepare Chilled Cucumber-Watercress Soup.
2. Steam potatoes.
3. Prepare salad.
4. Cook Currant-Glazed Lamb Chops.

Chilled Cucumber-Watercress Soup

2   cups sour cream, divided
$^1/_2$ cup milk
$^1/_2$ cup watercress sprigs
2   medium cucumbers, peeled
      and coarsely chopped
4   teaspoons lemon juice
$^1/_4$ cup chopped onion
$^1/_2$ teaspoon salt
$^1/_8$ teaspoon pepper
      Watercress for garnish

In blender combine 1$^1/_2$ cups sour cream with remaining ingredients except watercress reserved for garnish. Puree. Pour into bowl or jar and chill in freezer until serving time. Garnish with reserved watercress and dollop of sour cream.

Currant-Glazed Lamb Chops

$^3/_4$ cup red currant jelly
$^1/_3$ cup water
6   loin lamb chops (12 if
      small), about 1$^1/_2$ inches
      thick

Preheat broiler. In small saucepan melt currant jelly with water over low heat. Remove from heat; set aside. Broil chops 2 to 3 inches from heat 5 to 6 minutes, until browned. Turn and broil other side 5 minutes. Brush chops with melted jelly and broil 1 minute. Turn, brush with glaze again and broil 1 minute longer.

Green Salad with Romano Dressing

$^3/_4$ cup grated Romano cheese
$^2/_3$ cup salad oil
1   garlic clove, pressed
3   tablespoons vinegar
2   heads Bibb lettuce
1   green pepper, cut into
      chunks
1   medium red onion, sliced
      and separated into rings

In jar with tight-fitting lid combine cheese, oil, garlic and vinegar. Combine lettuce, pepper chunks and onion rings in salad bowl. Shake dressing vigorously and toss with salad.

BROILED LAMB CHOP TIPS

• *Buy chops 1$^1/_2$ inches thick, broil 2 to 3 inches from heat and follow this guide: for rare lamb, 3 to 4 minutes each side; for medium, 5 to 6 minutes each side.*

• *Lamb chops are best when at least slightly rare; don't overcook them.*

Fillet of Sole with Grapes

A SEAFOOD DINNER IN THE FRENCH TRADITION

In France the word "Veronique" is used to designate entrees featuring grapes. This dish is a version of the popular Sole Veronique, served in a sauce tangy with lemon juice. The dessert, also French, has its own beguiling sauce.

Menu for 6

- **Fillet of Sole with Grapes Rice**
- **Asparagus with Dill Butter Sauce**
- **Peaches Sabayon**

SHOPPING LIST

- □ 1½ pounds fresh or frozen sole fillets
- □ 2 pounds fresh asparagus
- □ ¾ pound seedless green grapes
- □ 3 lemons
- □ 1½ pounds fresh peaches
- □ 1 kiwi fruit (optional)
- □ 1 bunch fresh dill or dillweed
- □ 1 8-ounce container plain yogurt
- □ ½ pint heavy or whipping cream
- □ 1 small bottle peach or apricot brandy

Have on Hand
- □ Long-grain rice
- □ Sugar

- □ Garlic
- □ Chives
- □ Dried bread crumbs
- □ Grated Parmesan cheese
- □ Butter or margarine
- □ Eggs
- □ Mayonnaise

SCHEDULE

1. Cook rice.
2. Prepare Fillets of Sole with Grapes.
3. Slice fruit and prepare sauce for dessert; chill separately.
4. Prepare Asparagus with Dill Butter Sauce.

Fillet of Sole with Grapes

2	eggs, slightly beaten
1/3	cup plain yogurt
3	tablespoons chopped chives
3	tablespoons mayonnaise
1½	pounds fresh or frozen sole fillets
3	tablespoons lemon juice
½	garlic clove, minced
3/4	pound seedless green grapes
1/3	cup dried bread crumbs
2	tablespoons grated Parmesan cheese
1	lemon, cut into wedges

Preheat oven to 400° F. In small bowl combine eggs, yogurt, chives and mayonnaise. With serrated knife cut fish into 1-inch chunks. In medium bowl combine fish, lemon juice and minced garlic. Add grapes; toss. Spoon fish and grapes into six individual baking shells or a square baking dish. Spoon yogurt mixture over fish; sprinkle with bread crumbs and Parmesan. Bake 12 to 15 minutes until hot and bubbly. Garnish with lemon wedges.

Asparagus with Dill Butter Sauce

2	pounds fresh asparagus, trimmed
1/4	teaspoon salt
1/4	cup butter or margarine
2	tablespoons finely chopped fresh dill or about 1½ teaspoons dried dillweed

In medium saucepan cook asparagus in boiling salted water to cover 5 to 7 minutes, just until tender-crisp; drain well. Return to saucepan with butter or margarine and dill. Heat until butter melts.

Peaches Sabayon

4	egg yolks
1/4	cup sugar
1/4	cup peach or apricot brandy
1/2	cup heavy or whipping cream
1½	pounds fresh peaches, peeled and sliced
1	kiwi fruit, peeled and sliced (optional)

In top of double boiler combine egg yolks and sugar. Beat until blended. In small saucepan warm brandy. Whisk into egg mixture. Set over simmering water and beat until thickened. Place in freezer.

Whip cream until soft peaks form; fold into sauce. Spoon peaches and kiwi into 6 dessert dishes. Top with sauce.

FRENCH FISH FILLETS

Here are some of the French styles for serving fillets of sole.
- Florentine: *On a bed of spinach*
- Marinière: *In a white wine sauce and, properly, garnished with mussels*
- Meunière: *Lightly floured, sauteed in butter and sprinkled with lemon juice*
- À la Provençal: *With tomato and garlic*

Saltimbocca

A MEAL FLAVORED WITH SAGE AND BASIL

Use fresh basil, with its subtle yet delicious flavor, for this unique tomato salad. Fresh herbs will enhance the Saltimbocca, too. End this very special meal with cool and tangy lemon sherbet.

Menu for 6

- **Tomatoes and Mozzarella with Basil**
- **Saltimbocca**
  Fresh Broccoli
  Italian Bread

Lemon Sherbet

SHOPPING LIST

- ☐ 6 chicken cutlets
- ☐ 6 thin slices prosciutto
- ☐ 1 bunch fresh broccoli
- ☐ 2 medium tomatoes
- ☐ 1 small red onion
- ☐ 1 bunch fresh basil
- ☐ 1 bunch fresh sage or dried sage
- ☐ 2 lemons
- ☐ 1 8-ounce package semisweet chocolate
- ☐ 1 loaf Italian bread
- ☐ 8 ounces mozzarella cheese
- ☐ 1 8-ounce container whipped topping made with real cream
- ☐ 1 quart lemon sherbet

Have on Hand

- ☐ Sugar
- ☐ Salt
- ☐ Pepper
- ☐ Garlic
- ☐ Olive oil
- ☐ Salad oil
- ☐ Red wine vinegar
- ☐ Butter or margarine
- ☐ Dry white wine

SCHEDULE

1. Prepare Saltimbocca.
2. Cook broccoli.
3. Prepare Tomatoes and Mozzarella with Basil.

Tomatoes and Mozzarella with Basil

½ cup fresh basil, coarsely chopped
1 small clove garlic
½ cup olive oil
2 tablespoons red wine vinegar
½ teaspoon sugar
½ teaspoon salt
Dash pepper
2 medium tomatoes, sliced ¼-inch thick
8 ounces mozzarella cheese, sliced ¼-inch thick
½ small red onion, sliced ¼-inch thick and separated into rings
Whole basil leaves

In blender or food processor combine basil, garlic, oil, vinegar, sugar, salt and pepper; blend until smooth.

Arrange alternate slices of tomato and cheese on platter; top with onion rings. Just before serving, drizzle with dressing and garnish with whole basil leaves.

Saltimbocca

6 chicken cutlets
Pepper
12 fresh sage leaves or 1½ teaspoons dried

6 thin slices prosciutto or Virginia ham, cut in half
3 tablespoons butter or margarine, divided
1½ tablespoons salad oil
½ cup dry white wine

Place chicken cutlets between sheets of wax paper and pound to ¼-inch thickness. Cut each cutlet in half; sprinkle lightly with pepper. Place 1 sage leaf or ⅛ teaspoon dried sage on each piece. Top with prosciutto or ham slice and secure horizontally with toothpicks.

In large heavy skillet melt 1 tablespoon butter or margarine with the oil. Add half the chicken and brown over medium-high heat 3 to 4 minutes on each side. Place on serving dish; remove picks and keep chicken warm. Repeat with remaining chicken, adding another tablespoon butter. Remove chicken and add wine to skillet; cook over high heat, scraping up browned bits, until slightly thickened. Remove from heat and swirl in remaining tablespoon butter. Pour over chicken.

FRESH BASIL TIPS

The taste of basil is clovelike, rich, warm and slightly peppery.
- *Use it in egg and tomato dishes and salads.*
- *Blend it with oil, cheese and nuts for pesto.*
- *Add it to fish and shellfish entrees.*
- *You can freeze basil in clean, dry plastic bags. The leaves may darken, but the flavor stays true.*

Pork Cutlets with Cider Sauce

PORK AND APPLES—A NATURAL FOR AUTUMN

Now that boneless cutlets are widely available, the wide variety of pork entrees are easier to prepare and require less cooking time. This one has a brisk cidery sauce. Pair it with a cool and fruity salad and a fast combination vegetable.

Menu for 6

- **Pork Cutlets with Cider Sauce**
- **Orange-Endive Salad**

Carrots and Brussels Sprouts

Pumpkin or Mince Pie

SHOPPING LIST

- ☐ 12 pork loin cutlets
- ☐ 1 pound carrots
- ☐ 2 10-ounce container fresh Brussels sprouts or 2 10-ounce packages frozen sprouts
- ☐ 2 heads Bibb or Boston lettuce
- ☐ 3/4 pound Belgian endive
- ☐ 1 bunch parsley
- ☐ 2 large apples
- ☐ 1 13³/4- or 14¹/2-ounce can chicken broth
- ☐ 1 11-ounce can mandarin oranges
- ☐ 1 small jar apple jelly
- ☐ Pumpkin or mince pie

Have on Hand
- ☐ Cornstarch
- ☐ Salt
- ☐ Pepper
- ☐ Olive oil
- ☐ Cider vinegar
- ☐ Wine vinegar
- ☐ Butter or margarine
- ☐ Apple cider or juice

SCHEDULE

1. Prepare Pork Cutlets with Cider Sauce.
2. Prepare Carrots and Brussels Sprouts.
3. Prepare salad.

Pork Cutlets with Cider Sauce

12	pork loin cutlets
1/4	teaspoon salt
1/8	teaspoon pepper
3	tablespoons butter or margarine
2	tablespoons cider vinegar
1 1/2	cups apple cider or juice
1 1/2	tablespoons apple jelly
1/3	cup chicken broth
1 1/2	teaspoons cornstarch
3	tablespoons water
2	large apples, unpeeled, sliced

Place cutlets between sheets of wax paper and pound to 1/4-inch thickness. Season with salt and pepper. In heavy skillet melt butter or margarine over medium heat. Add cutlets 2 or 3 at a time and cook until lightly browned, 3 to 5 minutes on each side. Remove from skillet; cover and set aside. Add vinegar to skillet, scrape up browned bits, and cook until almost all liquid has evaporated. Add apple cider or juice, jelly and chicken broth. Cook over high heat until sauce is reduced to about 1 cup, approximately 5 minutes. In cup dissolve cornstarch in water. Add to sauce and cook over medium-high heat, stirring constantly until thickened, about 1 minute. Lower heat and add apple slices and cutlets to sauce, turning cutlets to coat both sides. Cover and simmer 2 minutes or until apples are tender.

Orange-Endive Salad

2	heads Bibb or Boston lettuce
3/4	pound Belgian endive
1	can (11 oz.) mandarin oranges, drained
3 1/2	tablespoons chopped parsley, divided
4 1/2	tablespoons olive oil
1 1/2	tablespoons wine vinegar
1/4	teaspoon salt
	Dash pepper

Line salad bowl with lettuce. Add endive and mandarin oranges. Sprinkle with 1 1/2 tablespoons parsley. Combine rest of parsley and remaining ingredients and drizzle over salad.

OTHER TASTY PORK COMBINATIONS

Pork tastes good with fruit as well as with vegetables. It's delicious with glazed peach or apricot halves, pineapple slices and sauteed apples. It seems to team best with such strong-flavored vegetables as cabbage, cauliflower, Brussels sprouts, leeks, turnips, parsnips and rutabaga.

Linguine with Blender Pesto Sauce

PERFECT PASTA DINNER FOR GUESTS

This quick and easy pesto will keep for a week in the refrigerator, so make a double batch if you wish. And remember—fresh basil is a must.

Menu for 6

Smoked Trout or Whitefish with Crackers
• **Linguine with Blender Pesto Sauce**

Tossed Green Salad with
• **Roquefort Vinaigrette**
Garlic Parsley Bread

• **Quick Tortoni**

SHOPPING LIST

- ☐   Smoked trout or whitefish
- ☐   Salad greens
- ☐ 1 bunch fresh parsley
- ☐ 1 bunch fresh basil
- ☐ 1 jar pine nuts
- ☐ 1 16-ounce package linguine
- ☐ 1 8-ounce can fruit cocktail
- ☐ 1 small can or package pecans
- ☐ 1 small package macaroons
- ☐ 1 loaf French bread
- ☐   Crackers
- ☐ 2 ounces Roquefort or blue cheese
- ☐ 1 pint vanilla ice cream
- ☐   Peach-flavored brandy

Have on Hand

- ☐ Salt
- ☐ Pepper
- ☐ Olive oil
- ☐ Garlic
- ☐ Salad oil
- ☐ Red wine vinegar
- ☐ Parmesan cheese

SCHEDULE

1. Prepare Quick Tortoni.
2. Prepare Linguine with Blender Pesto Sauce.
3. Prepare Tossed Green Salad with Roquefort Vinaigrette.

Linguine with Blender Pesto Sauce

¾ pound linguine
   Salt
2 cups tightly packed basil leaves
1 cup olive oil
4 tablespoons pine nuts
2 garlic cloves
½ cup grated Parmesan cheese

Cook linguine in boiling salted water according to package directions; drain well. Meanwhile, combine basil, oil, pine nuts, garlic and a dash of salt in blender. Blend on high speed until smooth. Pour into serving bowl and stir in Parmesan. Let stand at room temperature a few minutes. Serve over linguine.

Roquefort Vinaigrette

1 teaspoon salt
¼ teaspoon pepper
¼ cup red wine vinegar
¼ cup water
¼ cup olive oil
¼ cup salad oil
¼ cup crumbled Roquefort or blue cheese

In jar with tight-fitting lid combine salt, pepper, wine vinegar and water; cover and shake. Add oils; cover and shake again. Add crumbled cheese and let stand at room temperature until serving time. Shake again before tossing with salad. Store leftover dressing in refrigerator.

Quick Tortoni

1 pint vanilla ice cream, softened
1 can (8 oz.) fruit cocktail, well drained
½ cup crumbled macaroons
⅓ cup chopped pecans, toasted
⅓ cup peach-flavored brandy

Line 8 muffin pan cups with paper liners. In large bowl combine all ingredients. Stir to blend. Spoon into muffin cups and cover with plastic wrap. Place in freezer until serving time. Serve extras as seconds or snacks.

A VARIATION ON VINAIGRETTE

To make Herb Vinaigrette, substitute tarragon vinegar for wine vinegar in Roquefort Vinaigrette recipe above. Instead of crumbled cheese, add 1 teaspoon each dried dill, basil and chopped parsley and 1 crushed garlic clove. Delicious on any green vegetable salad.

Turkey Gumbo

DELICIOUS DOWN-HOME DINNER

Starting with the fried oysters, your family and guests will know they're in for a hearty treat. Serve the gumbo piping hot in a tureen with a basket of warm, fragrant muffins nearby, and watch this good hearty food vanish before your eyes.

═ Menu for 6 ═

- **Fried Oysters**   **Corn Muffins**
- **Turkey Gumbo**   **Green Salad**
- **Praline Sundaes**

SHOPPING LIST

- ☐ 1   quart shucked oysters
- ☐ ½   pound cooked turkey
- ☐   Salad greens
- ☐ 1   green pepper
- ☐ 1   bunch celery
- ☐ 1   medium onion
- ☐ 1   bunch fresh parsley
- ☐ 2   13¾- or 14½-ounce cans chicken broth
- ☐ 1   16-ounce can tomatoes
- ☐ 1   jar tartar sauce
- ☐ 1   jar butterscotch topping
- ☐ 1   small package praline candy
- ☐ 1   small can or package pecan halves
- ☐   Corn muffins
- ☐ 1   10-ounce package frozen okra
- ☐ 1   quart vanilla ice cream

Have on Hand

- ☐   Long-grain rice
- ☐   Bread crumbs
- ☐   Salt
- ☐   Pepper
- ☐   Bay leaves
- ☐   Salad dressing
- ☐   Butter or margarine
- ☐   Eggs
- ☐   Worcestershire sauce

SCHEDULE

1. Cook Turkey Gumbo.
2. Prepare salad greens.
3. Prepare Fried Oysters.
4. Heat corn muffins.

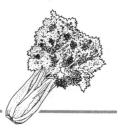

Fried Oysters

2   eggs
2   pints shucked oysters,
        drained
1   cup dried bread crumbs
¹/₂ cup butter or margarine
     Tartar sauce

In small bowl beat eggs lightly with fork. Dip oysters in eggs, then in bread crumbs. In large skillet heat butter or margarine until it sizzles. Add oysters and fry until golden brown. Spear with toothpicks and serve with tartar sauce.

Turkey Gumbo

2   tablespoons butter or
        margarine
1   medium onion, diced
¹/₃ cup diced green pepper
2   ribs celery, sliced
2   cans (13³/₄ or 14¹/₂ oz.
        each) chicken broth
1   can (16 oz.) tomatoes,
        undrained
¹/₂ teaspoon salt
¹/₈ teaspoon pepper
¹/₃ cup uncooked long-grain
        rice
1   cup frozen cut okra
2   cups diced cooked turkey
2   tablespoons chopped
        parsley
1   bay leaf
     Dash Worcestershire sauce

In large saucepot melt butter or margarine and brown onion and pepper. Add remaining ingredients and bring to a boil. Cover and reduce heat; simmer until vegetables and rice are tender, about 20 minutes. Remove bay leaf and serve.

Praline Sundaes

1   quart vanilla ice cream
³/₄ cup butterscotch topping
6   tablespoons crumbled
        praline candy
12 pecan halves

Place one or two scoops ice cream in each dessert dish. Top each with butterscotch topping, 1 tablespoon crumbled pralines and 2 pecan halves.

MAKE YOUR OWN TARTAR SAUCE

Mix together 1 cup mayonnaise, 2 or 3 tablespoons chopped sweet pickle, 2 tablespoons grated or minced onion, 1 tablespoon chopped fresh parsley and 1 or 2 teaspoons lemon juice.

Sauteed Chicken Portuguese

CHICKEN WITH A HINT OF NOUVELLE CUISINE

Tomatoes and fennel lend a distinctive flavor to this quick chicken dish. As its name tells you, the dessert is definitely au courant.

═══ Menu for 6 ═══

- **Sauteed Chicken Portuguese Stuffing with Onion and Parsley**

- **Braised Carrots and Celery with Basil**
- **Nouvelle Sundaes**

SHOPPING LIST

- ☐ 2 broiler fryers (about 2½ pounds each), cut up
- ☐ 4 tomatoes
- ☐ 2 onions
- ☐ 1 pound carrots
- ☐ 1 bunch celery
- ☐ 1 bunch fresh basil
- ☐ 1 bunch fresh parsley
- ☐ 2 kiwi fruit
- ☐ 1 package stuffing mix
- ☐ 1 quart raspberry sherbet
- ☐ Black raspberry liqueur or brandy

Have on Hand
- ☐ All-purpose flour

- ☐ Butter or margarine
- ☐ Salt
- ☐ Pepper
- ☐ Salad oil
- ☐ Fennel seed
- ☐ Dry white wine

SCHEDULE

1. Prepare Sauteed Chicken Portuguese.
2. Prepare Stuffing with Onion and Parsley.
3. Prepare Braised Celery with Basil.
4. Peel kiwi fruit for sundaes.

Sauteed Chicken Portuguese

1	cup all-purpose flour
1	teaspoon salt
¼	teaspoon pepper
2	broiler/fryers (2½ lbs. each), cut up
4	tablespoons salad oil
1½	cups dry white wine
1	onion, sliced
¾	teaspoon fennel seed
4	tomatoes, quartered and seeded
	Parsley sprigs

In plastic or paper bag combine flour, salt and pepper. Add chicken and shake to coat a few pieces at a time. In large skillet brown chicken in oil, turning occasionally, 15 minutes. Add wine, onion and fennel seed. Cook about 10 minutes until chicken is tender. Add tomato wedges and cook until heated through. Garnish with parsley sprigs.

Braised Carrots and Celery with Basil

1	pound carrots, peeled and sliced
3	ribs celery, sliced
¾	cup water
½	teaspoon salt
2	teaspoons chopped fresh basil or ½ teaspoon dried

1	tablespoon butter or margarine

Place carrots, celery and water in skillet. Cover and simmer 5 to 8 minutes or until vegetables are tender-crisp. Drain and toss with salt, basil and butter or margarine.

Nouvelle Sundaes

1	quart raspberry sherbet
6	tablespoons black raspberry liqueur or brandy
2	kiwi fruit, peeled and sliced

Place 1 scoop sherbet in each dessert dish. Top with 1 tablespoon liqueur or brandy. Garnish with several slices of kiwi.

LEFTOVER CELERY? STUFF IT WITH . . .

- *Peanut butter and a scattering of sunflower seeds*
- *Guacamole and chopped green chilies*
- *1 small can deviled ham mixed with ½ teaspoon curry powder and 2 tablespoons butter*
- *Softened Gorgonzola or Cheddar cheese flecked with minced parsley*
- *Cream cheese spread with chutney and a topping of slivered almonds*
- *1 can minced clams (drained), cream cheese and snips of dill.*

Deli Spread

A COOL MENU FOR SUMMER ENTERTAINING

Here is a no-cooking meal suitable for either a sit-down dinner or a buffet luncheon. See our Tips section for ideas.

═══ Menu for 6 ═══

- **Garden Vegetable Dip with Cherry Tomatoes and Celery Sticks**
- **Deli Spread**

Rye Bread
Strawberries with Creme Fraiche and Brown Sugar

SHOPPING LIST

- ☐ 6 to 8 ounces thinly sliced roast beef
- ☐ 6 to 8 ounces thinly sliced Virginia ham
- ☐ 6 to 8 ounces sliced turkey
- ☐ 1 head lettuce
- ☐ 1 small onion
- ☐ 1 bunch radishes
- ☐ 1 bunch celery
- ☐ 1 pint cherry tomatoes
- ☐ 1 carrot
- ☐ 2 pints strawberries
- ☐ 6 to 8 ounces thinly sliced Swiss or Muenster cheese
- ☐ 6 to 8 ounces Cheddar cheese
- ☐ 1 loaf rye bread
- ☐ 1 8-ounce package cream cheese
- ☐ 1 8-ounce container sour cream
- ☐ 1 8-ounce container creme fraiche

Have on Hand

- ☐ Salt
- ☐ Pepper
- ☐ Brown sugar
- ☐ 1 lemon or lemon juice
- ☐ Mayonnaise
- ☐ Horseradish

SCHEDULE

1. Prepare Garden Vegetable Dip.
2. Prepare Horseradish Mayonnaise and Russian Dressing.
3. Arrange Deli Spread platter.

Garden Vegetable Dip

1   package (8 oz.) cream
     cheese, softened
2½   tablespoons sour cream
2   tablespoons minced onion
2   tablespoons minced
     radish
½   cup grated carrot
¼   teaspoon salt
3   drops lemon juice
     cherry tomatoes
     celery sticks

In medium bowl beat cream cheese with sour cream. Stir in onion, radish, carrot, salt and lemon juice. Serve with cherry tomatoes and celery sticks.

Deli Spread

8   ounces thinly sliced roast
     beef
8   ounces thinly sliced
     Virginia ham
8   ounces sliced turkey
8   ounces thinly sliced Swiss
     or Muenster cheese
8   ounces Cheddar cheese
1   head lettuce
1   cup mayonnaise
2   tablespoons sour cream
2   tablespoons horseradish

Arrange meats and cheeses on lettuce leaves on large serving platter.

In small bowl combine mayonnaise, sour cream and horseradish. Serve with meats and cheeses.

COLD MEAT AND CHEESE PLATTER SUGGESTIONS

- *Offer thinly sliced Jarslberg cheese, Monterey Jack or Gjetost instead of Swiss and Cheddar.*
- *In place of the usual roast beef, ham and turkey, serve sliced salami, olive loaf and bologna.*
- *Serve 2 or more breads with the meal—rye and white, for example, or pumpernickel and whole wheat rolls.*
- *Offer a variety of condiments such as Russian dressing, Dijon-style mustard, chili sauce and ketchup.*
- *Serve dill and sweet pickles with ripe and green olives.*
- *Garnish the meat and cheese platter with fresh parsley, watercress, fresh dill or tomato wedges.*
- *Serve a generous bowl of deli macaroni salad, potato salad or cole slaw.*

Index

For information on how to subscribe to
Ladies' Home Journal, please write to:

Ladies' Home Journal
Subscription Dept.
P.O. Box #6034
Palm Coast, FL 32037